BREAD

BREAD

A Memoir of Hunger

Lisa Knopp

UNIVERSITY OF MISSOURI PRESS
Columbia

Copyright © 2016 by
The Curators of the University of Missouri
University of Missouri Press, Columbia, Missouri 65211
Printed and bound in the United States of America
All rights reserved. First printing, 2016.

ISBN: 978-0-8262-2102-5
Library of Congress Control Number: 2016951041

∞™ This paper meets the requirements of the
American National Standard for Permanence of Paper
for Printed Library Materials, Z39.48, 1984.

Typefaces: Minion Pro, Univers

The names and identifying characteristics of some individuals in this book have
been changed to protect the privacy of those involved.

Once again, for my mother, Patricia Parris Knopp (1935–2016), my greatest fan, with love, appreciation, and gratitude

CONTENTS

PREFACE

A few years ago, I found it very easy and very gratifying to tightly restrict what, when, and how much I ate. It was with a sense of triumph and delight that I watched myself becoming smaller and taking up less space. A whisper, a shadow, or a flicker is what I wanted to be. When I finally realized that the disordered eating that had left me sick and small when I was fifteen and again when I was twenty-five had returned when I was deep into middle age, I was full of urgent questions. Why did I respond to that which threatened or overwhelmed me by restricting my food intake? How can one heal from a condition that is the result of a tangle of genetic, biological, psychological, economic, and cultural forces? Are eating disorders and disordered eating in older women caused by the same factors as in younger women? Or are they caused, in part, by the sorrows and frustrations of aging in a culture that sees midlife and beyond as a time of inexorable decline marked by increasing deterioration, powerlessness, dependency, and irrelevance and so marginalizes older people? In my search for answers to these questions, I read studies by experts on eating disorders and revisited those dark periods in my life when reducing myself to skin and bones seemed like the best antidote to whatever was ailing me.

This book is the account of my efforts to understand the causes and nature of this perplexing and recurring problem in my life. In the introduction, I define terms, chiefly noting the difference between an eating disorder, which is a psychological illness and has a clinical diagnosis, and disordered eating, which is an abnormal or maladapted relationship with food, weight, body image, and self. I suspect that most women and too many men and children in our culture, obsessed as it is with appearances and possessions over substance, soul, and spirit, experience the symptoms of disordered eating. In "The Punishing Summer," "Other Kitchens, Other Tables," and "The Gray Years" (chapters 1, 3, and 4), I view disordered eating from the inside out by recounting the tales of my first and second serious bouts with my malady (when I was fifteen, I restricted myself to fewer than six hundred calories per day; because of a food phobia when I was in my mid-twenties, I could eat only under tightly controlled circumstances). In "White Bread" (chapter 2), I consider bread as physical substance, as industrial marvel, as countercultural symbol of what was corrupt and shallow about the dominant, mainstream culture, and as spiritual metaphor. In "Nurture," "Hardwired," and "Cravings" (chapters 5, 6, and 7), the more scholarly part of the book, I present some of the theories about the familial, biological, environmental, cultural, and spiritual causes of eating disorders and disordered eating and the solutions they offer people who stuff or starve themselves in an attempt to satisfy their yearnings for love, security, identity, purpose, and meaning. In "Full" (chapter 8), I focus on the relatively normal eating and thinking that I enjoyed during my thirties, forties, and early fifties, years when I was consumed by the demands of single parenting my two children, as well as teaching, writing, and maintaining a home. In "The Grieving Season" and "The Third Choice" (chapters 9 and 10), I delve into the story of the unexpected return of my malady in my mid-fifties, when I responded to a cluster of separations and losses that left me feeling sad, empty, and hopeless by restricting my food intake, and the ways I eventually discovered to feed my deepest hungers.

I have many hopes for this book. I hope to convince readers that eating disorders and disordered eating are about more than just food and weight. I hope that the story of my malady and my search for understanding will inform and inspire those who also suffer from a conflicted relationship with food, weight, and self-image. Because eating disorders and disordered eating among older women are more common than most people realize, I hope to raise awareness about this hidden, little-studied, little-discussed phenomenon. I hope that those who eat normally and aren't preoccupied with the number on the bathroom scale will find something in my story and reflections that speaks to them, too, since this is not only a food memoir and an illness narrative but a spiritual autobiography, concerned as it is with various appetites, hungers, desires, nourishments, and fulfillments.

Most books about eating disorders and disordered eating are written by medical doctors or psychologists, or by those who have been diagnosed with anorexia nervosa, bulimia nervosa, or binge-eating disorder and treated by specialists in residential programs. I am none of these. I am a writer and this book is a work of creative nonfiction, a first-person account of one woman's illness and what she learned about herself and her culture because of it. For those who are restricting, binging, or binging and purging or for those who are concerned about someone who is, no part of this book or my story is to be taken as a substitute for consultation with a medical or mental health professional.

ACKNOWLEDGMENTS

I gratefully acknowledge those institutions and individuals that generously supported me in various ways during the writing of this memoir: *Rock & Sling: A Journal of Witness,* which published "My Daily Bread" in issue 11 (Spring 2016); the Kimmel Nelson Harding Center for the Arts in Nebraska City, Nebraska, for awarding me a three-week residency in January 2015; the Nebraska Arts Council for awarding me a $2,500 Distinguished Artist Award (creative nonfiction) through the 2015 Individual Artist Fellowship Awards in Literature program; the University of Nebraska–Omaha for awarding me a sabbatical for the spring semester of 2015; and David Rosenbaum, Clair Willcox, Mary S. Conley, Sara Davis, Stephanie L. Williams, Deanna Davis, Drew Griffith, and all the others at the University of Missouri Press for their contributions.

I am more grateful than I can ever say to my editor, Gloria Thomas, my daughter, Meredith Ezinma Ramsay, and my mother, Patricia Knopp, who helped me to understand myself, my malady, and how to present my story.

BREAD

MY MALADY

AN INTRODUCTION

When I tell people that I have written a memoir about my conflicted relationship with food, many of them tell me stories about being in the grip of something beyond their control that leads them to eat too much or too little, about feeling shamed or misunderstood or isolated because of their eating or not eating, about the familial or social tensions or the ill physical effects that have arisen because of their unhealthy relationship with food. Some of these storytellers meet the narrow diagnostic criteria for three of the eating disorders (anorexia nervosa, bulimia nervosa, and binge-eating disorder) listed in the *Diagnostic and Statistical Manual of Mental Disorders* (*DSM*), the diagnostic bible of the American Psychiatric Association. But most do not. Most have "disordered eating," which the authors of a 2009 study, "Patterns and Prevalence of Disordered Eating and Weight Control Behaviors in Women Ages 25–45," define as "unhealthy or maladaptive eating behaviors, such as restricting, binging, purging, or use of other compensatory behaviors, without meeting criteria for an eating disorder." "Maladaptive eating behaviors" include imbalanced eating (for instance, avoiding an entire food group like carbohydrates or fats; eating only foods that one deems "pure"; crash dieting; and alternating between binging and fasting). "Other compensatory behaviors" include the use of laxatives, diuretics, stimulants, or excessive exercise to counteract the calories one has consumed. But the stories people tell me about their disordered eating are about more than stuffing or starving. The deeper stories are about the tellers' feelings of unworthiness, emptiness, anxiety, self-consciousness, shame, or guilt. In short, they are stories about a hunger for wholeness and fullness.

Since most women, many men, and too many children in this time and place grapple with issues about eating, size, weight, and self-image, as well as the gnawing hungers that fuel these concerns, the story I tell and the stories I hear in response are common and representative. The authors of the 2009 study mentioned above found that of the women between the ages of twenty-five and forty-five that they surveyed, none of whom had a history of full-blown anorexia nervosa or bulimia nervosa, 31 percent reported using self-inflicted vomiting to control their weight, while 74.5 percent reported that their concerns about their shape and weight interfered with their happiness. "Normative discontent" is what psychologist Judith Rodin and her coauthors call the dissatisfaction that many people in economically developed countries feel about their body size, shape, and weight, even when their weight is normal. Apparently, "maladaptive eating behaviors" have also become normative. In *Almost Anorexic: Is My (or My Loved One's) Relationship with Food a Problem?*, Jennifer J. Thomas and Jenni Schaefer report that "for every adult who has experienced full syndrome anorexia (roughly 1 in 200), many more (at least 1 in 20) have struggled with *almost anorexia*" (italics mine).

Imagine a continuum of attitudes about food, eating, size, and weight. On one end are those who have a normal, healthy attitude toward food, which to me means eating when hungry, not eating when not hungry, having a positive body image, maintaining a stable weight, and not being preoccupied with thoughts of food, weight, and size. On the other end of the continuum are those with clinically defined and diagnosed eating disorders: anorexia nervosa, which the *DSM-5*, published in 2013, describes as being characterized by a "distorted body image and excessive dieting that leads to severe weight loss with a pathological fear of becoming fat"; bulimia nervosa, characterized by "frequent episodes of binge eating followed by inappropriate behaviors such as self-induced vomiting to avoid weight gain"; and binge-eating disorder, characterized by "recurring episodes of eating significantly more food in a short period of time than most people would eat under similar circumstances, with episodes marked by feelings of lack of control." Between these two poles is a wide gray area, where those who do not meet the diagnostic requirements for an eating disorder, yet manifest some of the same thoughts and behaviors as those who do, are located. These aren't fixed positions. Depending on what's going on in one's life, one might move closer either to the normal or to the more seriously disordered end of the continuum. Consequently, the line between normal and pathological thinking and behaviors related to eating, body size, and image isn't clear or set, with anorexia, bulimia, and binge-eating disorder but extreme versions of what many think about their bodies and of the behaviors those thoughts can lead to. Because "disordered eating" lies in the gray area, it is largely unrecognized and untreated.

Though we tend to think of disordered eating and eating disorders as problems that largely afflict white, affluent females in their teens or twenties, studies show otherwise. A growing number of researchers are studying disordered-eating behaviors among racial and ethnic minorities, lower socioeconomic groups, males, and older women. Eating disorders appear to be as prevalent among African Americans and Latinos as among whites, though the condition is more likely to be underreported or underdiagnosed in these populations. One study showed that among blacks, binge-eating disorder is the most common and anorexia the least common eating disorder, with bulimia occurring at about the same rate as the national average. African Americans and Latinos both seem to be protected from anorexia to some extent because their respective cultures don't prize thinness as much as the mainstream culture does. It's difficult to determine the percentage of males with eating disorders. In the past, experts believed that about 5 percent of those with eating disorders were male, but now experts report higher numbers. The organization Anorexia Nervosa and Related Eating Disorders, for instance, says that 10 percent of those with eating disorders are male, while the National Eating Disorders Association says that the number may be as high as 25 percent. For males, eating disorders are often connected with the desire for a muscular, athletic build. As with black females, bulimia and binge-eating disorder are more common among males than anorexia.

In recent years, the number of older women seeking help for eating disorders has risen sharply, though it's not clear whether this indicates that there is an increase in the occurrence of the disorder, that general practitioners have become better at identifying it in this population, or that a larger percentage of those afflicted are seeking help. A study published in the July 2012 issue of the *International Journal of Eating Disorders* by Cynthia M. Bulik, director of the Center of Excellence for Eating Disorders at the University of North Carolina, and her coauthors found that based on responses to an online survey, women over fifty engage in disordered-eating behaviors *to the same extent* that adolescents do.

When I was deep into middle age, a professor at a state university, the author of five books and many dozens of essays, some of which had won national awards, and the mother of an adult son and daughter, I watched my weight drop to a number on the bathroom scale that I hadn't seen since seventh grade as I whittled down the list of foods that I could eat until it fit on my thumbnail. Because of age-related changes in my body, mind, and health and the departure of my adult children, I felt that I had lost so much. In spite of my successes, I was rigidly restricting what and how much I ate as a way of exerting what felt like power and control. I didn't know that I was sick again until my twenty-year-old daughter told me that if I didn't eat more, I was going to die. What astonishes me is that I was blind to what was happening to me during what I now call the "Grieving Season" and that I couldn't link it with the two other times when eating very little became so easy and satisfying for me.

During the "Punishing Summer" of 1972, when I was fifteen, I restricted my caloric intake to fewer than six hundred calories per day. I chewed and spit food, exercised excessively, lost weight so fast that I was anemic, stopped menstruating, and felt weighed down by the feeling that I wasn't good enough to win anyone's approval. I had never heard of anorexia nervosa, nor had the pediatrician who examined me when I was my thinnest and most unhealthy. But soon, there would be an explosion of books and articles about it, most notably Hilde Bruch's book *Eating Disorders: Obesity, Anorexia Nervosa, and the Person Within* in 1973 and *Time* magazine's article "The Self-Starvers" about the "Twiggy syndrome" in 1975. Apparently what happened to me during the Punishing Summer was surprisingly widespread among teenagers and young women in the United States. When I learned about anorexia years after I had experienced some of the symptoms of it, I saw that I had exhibited three of the four diagnostic features of the disorder listed in the third edition of the *DSM*, published in 1980. But I hadn't met the stringent weight requirement. Even though I'd lost well over 20 percent of my body weight in about two months, I weighed too much to "qualify."

When I was in my mid- and late twenties, I had an anxiety-based food phobia that made my life very difficult. I was afraid that if I ate food that other people had touched, I might be dosed with alcohol or dangerous drugs without my knowledge. To keep myself safe, I hid my food in my clothes closet and rarely ate anything that I hadn't prepared myself under carefully controlled conditions. I was eating less than my body needed to maintain my weight, as I had during the Punishing Summer, not to lose weight but to keep myself safe from all that I thought was trying to sabotage me during a time in my life in which I felt overwhelmed by everything, from the demanding new high school teaching position for which I felt poorly prepared to the new home and circle of friends that I was trying to create in a big city far from home, family, and friends. I call this period the "Gray Years" because the fear I felt surrounding the act of eating often left me feeling mentally paralyzed, frozen, or "fogged in."

To compare my different attitudes toward food during each of these episodes, let's imagine a slice of fresh strawberry pie topped with luscious whipped cream. During the Punishing Summer, I wouldn't eat the dessert simply because it contained so many calories, which would take up too many of the six hundred calories I'd allotted myself for each day and make me gain weight. During the Gray Years, I wouldn't eat the dessert because I would fear that someone had laced it with drugs or alcohol, which would make me lose control or cause brain damage. During the Grieving Season, I wouldn't eat the dessert because the graham cracker crust contains gluten, which causes gastrointestinal distress; in terms of pesticides, strawberries are the one of the "dirtiest" foods; the whipped cream is a sweet, fluffy mess of polysyllabic chemicals, none of which are good for you; and, depending on what else I'd eaten that day, the whole concoction might put me too close to my total number of allowable calories for the day, which I never, ever exceeded. Though my motivations would be different in each case, the outcome would be the same: denying myself a dessert that I love and believing that by tightly controlling what and how much I ate, I could conquer—or at least hold at bay—all that was trying to swallow me. No matter how you classify or name my episodes with disordered eating, the truth is this: though the angsts and challenges associated with each period were different, I turned to the same "solution," which was restricting what and how much I ate.

I have never received nor sought a clinical diagnosis for my disordered eating, though I suspect that the right name for what afflicts me would be "other specified feeding or eating disorder," a catchall or "other" category in the *DSM-5* that includes eating and feeding disorders of clinical severity that don't meet the diagnostic criteria for anorexia nervosa, bulimia nervosa, or binge-eating disorder. This category was called "eating disorders not otherwise specified" in the fourth edition of the *DSM*, published in 1994. Because I find these terms clunky and clinical, I do not refer to my condition as such. Nor do I refer to it as subthreshold, subclinical, atypical, partial-syndrome, or "almost" anorexia since those terms carry a value judgment—subpar, second rate, not up to snuff, bush league. If only I were to try a little harder. Instead, I refer to my three episodes of disordered eating and thinking collectively as my "malady," a word that is beautiful on the tongue—like a melody. This word is derived from the Latin *male*, which means "bad," and *habitus*, which is the past participle of the Latin *habere*, or "having," meaning "as a condition." *Malady* literally means "having a bad condition." Now we define the word more narrowly: "any disorder or disease of the body, especially one that is chronic or deep-seated." I find the contrast between the sound and the meaning of the word to be particularly appropriate since it suggests the contradictions and mystery, the pain and beauty of my malady, which matches my experiences of it.

Though I have had three episodes with my malady, it wasn't until the most recent one that it occurred to me that I should write about this confounding aspect of my life. The act of crafting this narrative and researching theories about the causes of and cures for my malady was filled with many moments of self-revelation since it demanded that I reexamine my long-held beliefs that my malady was due primarily to familial factors and innate personality traits, with some influence from the diet, fashion, beauty, and entertainment industries, which present a certain body type, and a very thin one at that, as ideal. Now I believe that disordered eating and eating disorders are due to a complex mix of genetic and biological factors, family dynamics, and a wide range of cultural, political, economic, and spiritual influences. This reassessment has prompted me to explore my malady as a protest against those American cultural values that I find ugly and destructive: the assumption that appearances matter more than substance; the belief that meaning, identity, and significance are found in the consumption of material commodities; the cultural backlash against the growing power and recognition of women during the past several decades; and, of particular concern with my third episode, the virulent form of ageism that renders a substantial portion of our population invisible and redundant. Though I tell the story of each of the three episodes of my malady, I am especially hopeful that my testimony, investigations, and reflections about the Grieving Season will draw attention to the easily overlooked or ignored link between disordered eating or eating disorders and aging.

The challenges I encountered in writing this book were many. While I have decades of therapy behind me and have talked, sometimes frankly, sometimes guardedly, with my therapists about my malady, and while I've chipped away at those thought patterns of mine that make eating very little and becoming small seem like such an appealing and reasonable solution to what punishes, threatens, or grieves me, I've never worked with a therapist who specializes in eating disorders. Nor am I an expert on the subject. How much have I gotten wrong or left out because I haven't yet read or heard or thought about it? How can I tell my personal story if I haven't finished reading the long list of books and articles by experts that I've compiled? Yet, even though I'm not as knowledgeable as I'd like to be about the cross-cultural research on eating disorders, or the recent studies regarding the brain chemistry and genetics behind the diseases, or about disordered-eating behaviors among males and ethnic and racial minority groups, those who have been sexually abused, athletes, people with diabetes, and other populations, having had three sustained and serious episodes with disordered eating does make me an expert of sorts. While I don't claim to be an authority, I do claim the authority to tell the story of my malady.

When people asked me what I was working on in my writing as I was crafting this memoir, I found myself embarrassed to say "a memoir about my disordered eating" or even the more benign "my conflicted relationship with food." Too many people see disordered eating or an eating disorder as a self-indulgence, a sign of weakness or lack of discipline, or an attempt to gain attention—in short, as a self-inflicted misery and the result of a character flaw or moral failing. Surely one would be cured of this silliness if only she'd get over herself, buck up, grow some backbone, or do some character-building, perspective-giving volunteer work, like serving soup at a homeless shelter to people who are truly hungry. Unfortunately, it's far easier to pass judgment on those who are suffering from something we don't understand than to open our hearts and minds to them and their story.

Another reason that I was reluctant to tell people what I was working on is the nature of illness narratives. G. Thomas Couser, in *Recovering Bodies:*

Illness, Disability, and Life Writing, juxtaposes a full-life narrative, a "comprehensive account of one's life into which one integrates the story of one's illness," with an "autopathography," which is limited to the story of an illness or disability. Because of the tight focus on one's illness in the latter, the autopathographer emphasizes what author and book reviewer Joyce Carol Oates calls "the sensational underside of its subject's life to the detriment of those more scattered, and less dramatic, periods of accomplishment and well being." The effect of this is a portrayal of the self that falls short of presenting a sound or fully functioning person. Yet Couser points out that while an autopathography can reinforce "conventional views" of an illness, it can also provide resistance to the dominant medical or cultural narrative and the stigmatization, patronization, and marginalization that often accompany illness or disability. That is empowering! To that end, I have attempted to go beyond a typical autopathography to tell a story about my experience of my malady that includes more than just personal disorder and dysfunction by attending to the cultural, political, and spiritual context in which the illness and the healing occur. For the most part, I've left out details about how many calories I consumed in a day and how many pounds I gained or lost since readers with eating disorders and disordered eating might read my memoir as an instructional or inspirational guidebook. I've also chosen not to disclose what I weighed since too many of us pass judgment on others based on their weight, whether too little, too much, or just right. While this memoir is primarily focused on the ebbs and flows of my malady, I've told a story, too, about my roles as daughter, teacher, mother, wife, divorced single parent, empty nester, spiritual seeker, political activist, professor, and writer.

This book was also challenging to write because those with disordered eating and eating disorders can be a pretty wily lot, prone to self-deception and subterfuge. We can't be trusted to view ourselves with clarity and insight. We find nothing odd about eating our precisely measured nibbles and bits or an entire carton of ice cream and then feeling that once again we've overdone it and spending the afternoon tallying and retallying our caloric intake and exercising for far too long to atone for our sins, obsessively checking our weight, and feeling like failures. We lie to others about what we have or haven't eaten; we lie to ourselves about who and what we see when we look in the mirror. What insanity or hubris is this for me to presume that I can write a sincere and unflinching account of my malady?

What parts of my story have I left out because they're too shameful or because I don't see them as significant or don't see them at all?

While I hope for a wide readership, the reader that I most clearly imagine is someone like me: an older female in need of answers. Consequently, I've written the type of book that would have been invaluable to me during the Grieving Season, which began in 2011, when I was sick and hungry and trying so hard to take up as little space as possible. My memoir moves between my personal story and my consideration of the most relevant theories and research on the causes and consequences of and the cures for disordered eating and eating disorders. The solution I discovered is simple though not easy.

I send this book into the world with reluctance. To share details about my inability to create and maintain a healthy relationship with something as basic as food is to admit that I, too, believe I'm guilty of a failure of will and character and have too little trust in God, who I believe can heal any and all of our sicknesses and restore us to wholeness. But I also send it into the world with the best of intentions: to share facts and truths about my malady to make myself and others a little freer. For this, I'm willing to be judged.

CHAPTER ONE

THE PUNISHING SUMMER

The only bread that I knew as a child was store bought, machine made, sliced, plastic wrapped, and white. My mother insisted that my two brothers and I eat a slice of the airy bread smeared with Blue Bonnet margarine as part of our supper. "Eat your bread and butter and then you can go play," she'd say, as if it were a green vegetable. "Crust, too. It's good for your teeth." The bread we usually ate came from the Sweetheart Bakery, our hometown bread factory. But sometimes, Dad, who did most of the grocery shopping, bought Wonder Bread, which I liked better because the TV commercial said that it was made from whipped batter, reminding me of cake, and that it "helped build strong bodies twelve ways." My favorite bread, however, was Sunbeam because the mascot, Little Miss Sunbeam, with her pink apple cheeks and her bouquet of golden ringlets bound with a blue bow on top of her head, looked so cherubic and happy as she ate her slice of buttered bread.

The first time I ate homemade bread may have been at my friend Ellen Lloyd's house, next door to mine. Unlike my mother and the women on her side of our family, Mrs. Lloyd didn't have a job outside the home. She filled her time by going to Catholic mass every day but Sunday, drinking lots of wine, and whipping up dishes I'd never heard of, like leek soup, and she made bread from scratch. She and her life seemed exotic to me—especially when she reminded us that she was from "the East." I knew that by that she didn't mean across the Mississippi River in Illinois, but somewhere much farther away and beyond my imagining. One time when I was hanging out at the Lloyd home with Ellen, probably fixing each other's hair as we listened to Carole King's "Tapestry" or James Taylor's "Sweet Baby James," Ellen gave me a slice of her mother's homemade bread. It had a mild, nutty flavor and a far more substantial texture than that of any bread I'd ever eaten. It was heavenly.

I clearly remember the first two times I made bread. Because of a scheduling glitch, the only elective that fit in my schedule in the after-lunch slot in ninth grade was Foods I, not something that I, an artsy kid, would have chosen. Mrs. Nye taught us to cook meat (she made us fry liver) and work with yeast (we made white bread and doughnuts). The three other girls in my kitchenette and I mixed the bread dough and then took turns pummeling it. So that we could wait until the next day to bake, we refrigerated the dough. Mrs. Nye came in that evening and punched it down. After my co-bakers and I pulled our loaves from the oven, Mrs. Nye nibbled a thin slice as she filled out an evaluation form about the crumb, crust, and flavor of our finished product. We received an A-. Then, in what little time remained in the class period, my co-bakers and I devoured generous slabs of the warm, buttered bread. The bread wasn't as white as Sweetheart bread, it had air holes of different sizes and a firmer, darker, chewier crust, and the slices were thick and uneven. It was divine. Both loaves were gone before the bell rang. Surely bread that had received a full A would have given me more pleasure than I could bear.

I loved homemade bread so much that I asked my father to pick up some yeast at the grocery store and I followed the recipe for "Enriched White Bread" in my mother's red-and-white plaid *Better Homes and Gardens New Cook Book.* The two loaves that I lifted from the oven were golden brown, fragrant, and disappointingly flat. When I looked at the recipe again, I realized why: instead of adding two teaspoons of salt, I'd added two tablespoons. I knew from Foods I that salt retards the reproductive activities of yeast by drawing moisture away from it, which is why my loaves were bricklike. Even so, I loved the heavier, grainier texture. I took part of a loaf to Mrs. Lloyd next door. She approved, but advised me to use less salt the next time.

When I was in sixth grade, I went through confirmation classes at our Methodist church. For my Palm Sunday confirmation, I wore panty hose for the first time and stood in front of the congregation with the rest of my class. Later that week, on Maundy Thursday, I took Communion for the first time. It was special going to church in the evening and seeing our beautiful, old sanctuary dimly lit. I was almost moved to tears by the solemnity and symbolism of the movements of our tall, black-robed pastor, the guy who wore pullover sweaters and joked with us at Saturday morning confirmation class, as he reenacted the Last Supper. He held up a loaf of bread and broke it, repeating Jesus's words: "This is my body given for you; do this in remembrance of me." At that moment, I was in the Upper Room with the disciples, watching a ritual that, like them, I didn't fully understand. The pastor invited the congregation to the Communion rail in groups. As we knelt, he served each of us a sip of grape juice in a tiny glass cup and a morsel of white bread.

I've always loved this rite of symbolic, communal eating and the idea that any given thing can stand for more than itself. In fact, that first Communion may have been when I fell in love with metaphor. The bread and juice were Jesus's flesh and blood. By eating and drinking this meal, I was taking Jesus into my body and soul. Communion offered a robust theological metaphor whose significance for me has grown with time. Now, when I place the Communion bread on my tongue, I am struck by the genius and the appropriateness of Jesus's presenting himself as something so common, so consumable, so essential, so nourishing as bread.

I'm not sure when I started binging on bread, but I associate it with babysitting. I had several regular, good-paying babysitting customers, and so from eighth grade until I left for college, I spent part of almost every weekend working. I wasn't particularly crazy about taking care of kids, though I did enjoy some of them, especially the younger ones. Rather, I needed money, and weekends were when I had time to work. Since several of my customers were educated professionals and seemed so affluent and sophisticated compared to so many of the people I knew in blue-collar Burlington, Iowa, I looked forward to going into their homes and seeing how they lived— the fashion boots in the closet, the pretty things in the bathroom, the albums they listened to (Simon & Garfunkel's *Bridge over Troubled Water* or the soundtrack of *Oh! Calcutta!*), and the books they read (*Portnoy's Complaint,* by Philip Roth, or the biography of Zelda Fitzgerald by Nancy Mitford).

After I put my charges to bed, I'd go in the kitchen and find the softest, moistest loaf of white bread. I'd take a couple of plain slices at a time—not from the ends, but from the softer middle of the loaf—fold them over, and scrunch them a bit so that they were condensed. When my mom made bread-and-butter sandwiches, she cut them into neat triangles, but my dad just buttered a slice and folded it in half—almost like what I did during my binges. It looked hurried and didn't taste as good as my mother's tidy triangles. My folding and scrunching of the bread was also hurried—urgent, even. I could have rolled the cushiony bread into a ball, but that was more firmness than I needed. During my binges, it wasn't the taste or density of the bread that I was after but the rhythm of stuffing the slices into my mouth, the chewing, the swallowing, and the stuffing, again and again. It was soothing, softening, blurring.

To sit at the table would have been to acknowledge what I was doing, and I didn't want my left hand to know what my right hand was doing. So I stood at the counter or knelt on the floor by the cupboard where I had found the bread and devoured a half loaf, one pair of slices after another. I may not have been hungry in my stomach, but somewhere, I was famished for something hard to name and impossible to find, and so I ate, secretively, ritualistically, alone. When I was at home, I could and did eat entire loaves of bread and then felt sick afterward from the bulk, the chemical additives, and my self-disgust. But not when I was babysitting. I figured that if I got caught, I'd rather get in trouble for eating a half rather than a whole loaf. Even then, though, I knew that binging on plain bread was not only bad but weird and that it would require more explaining than if I had wolfed down a package of Oreos or a box of Bugles.

For the duration of these binges, I was outside of myself, my mind no longer chewing on itself. Whatever I was hungry for could be satisfied, at least temporarily, by stuffing myself with bread.

By my sophomore year, my weight had ballooned to 135 pounds, far too much for my almost five-foot two-inch frame. Dark pink stretch marks scored the outer top part of my doughy thighs. In time, the marks turned a glossy, silvery white, reminding me of schools of slim, rippling fish. I usually wore bell-bottom blue jeans with a long pullover shirt or sweater to hide my hips and saddlebags, those fat bulges on the outside of my upper thighs. I wore the same regulation, snap-up-the-front blue gym suit that I'd gotten in seventh grade all through high school. But in tenth grade, it was uncomfortably, almost seam-splittingly tight in the thighs. On my way to and from the communal shower in physical education class, I was careful to hide my stretch marks with one of the tiny white towels that the teacher handed each of us.

One day I was standing in line for lunch in the cafeteria when my mom, who taught biology at the high school, walked past carrying her tray to the teacher's lounge. That evening she said she wanted to talk to me. She said that when she saw me standing in the lunch line at school, she was reminded of a time when she was in eighth grade. She hadn't realized how much weight she'd gained until she saw her reflection as she walked past a store window and saw her "bottom" sticking out like a shelf. She suggested that I start wearing a girdle so that my bottom wouldn't look as jiggly. That I was fat was obvious, yet I was embarrassed and ashamed when she named and spoke the problem. I could suck in my belly until it was flat, but there was nothing I could do about my butt and saddlebags. I wanted to grab handfuls of the flesh on my buttocks and thighs and pull or cut them off me.

I don't remember how I got my girdles. Most likely, my mother gave me a couple of hers. Or perhaps I used my babysitting money to buy them, though I can't imagine myself walking into J. C. Penney's and inquiring about such an item. Once I started wearing a girdle to school, I wore one every day since I would have felt underdressed without it. I figured out that when I wore a long-legged girdle, my stomach, butt, and saddlebags looked firmer and flatter, but when I wore a girdle that looked like a pair of waist-high underpants, my saddlebags looked even bulgier and more prominent. While I looked better in the long-legged girdle, I wore the panty girdle on those days that I had physical education class since it wasn't as obvious to the other girls what I was wearing when we changed into our gym suits. The first thing I would do when I returned home from school was wriggle out of my polyurethane prison, so that I was free and unrestrained, and then I would get a snack.

My mom also wore a girdle to work every day to firm her bottom and stomach. She was a yo-yo dieter, up and down, up and down, twenty or thirty or more pounds. She'd eat cottage cheese and tomato slices; she'd take ephedrine- and caffeine-loaded diet pills to rev up her metabolism; she and I both took the fiber-filled diet pills that swelled in your stomach so you'd get full faster. She tried various diets but lost the most weight on the Stillman high-protein, low-carbohydrate plan . . . and then gained it back. Every now and then, my mother would tell my father to pick up a vibrating-belt machine from the rental company. He'd set the machine in the basement near the washer and dryer. There, my mother would stand on the machine platform with the belt around her hips and jiggle away. The principle behind this machine was that it loosened or broke down the fat, which made it easier to flush it away. It heartened me to know that there was a way to get rid of fat without eating less and exercising more. I, too, tried to use the jiggle machine, but I found it unbearably boring since the motor was too loud for me to listen to the hit songs on Chicago's WLS and too jarring for me to hold a book in front of my face and focus on the words. I supposed that my mom and I never saw results, though, because we had to return the machine to the rental company before it had had enough time to blast the fat on our butts and thighs.

The girdles made me look firmer, but I was still too big. A fast and easy fix is what I wanted. I pored over magazine advertisements for Ayds, the "Reducing Plan Candy," which the ads promoted as a "safe and effective appetite suppressant" with amazing testimonials ("I barely fit in my bathtub, until I lost 74 pounds"). Far bigger people than me had dropped several dress sizes by eating Ayds, which came in chocolate, butterscotch, and caramel, with a hot drink an hour before each meal. "You eat less because you want less," the slim woman in the TV commercial assured me. If only I could get a box of Ayds, my weight would drop, my saddlebags would shrink, I'd be beautiful and popular, and my life at school and at home, less chaotic and frustrating. I never got to try the magical candies that would melt away my pounds and my worries. I figured that if I asked my parents to buy me a box of Ayds, they'd say no, and it never occurred to me that I could walk to the neighborhood drugstore and buy myself a box with my babysitting pay.

The summer following my sophomore year, my mother took graduate classes at the University of Iowa, which was eighty miles away. She lived in a dormitory during the week and came home on weekends. In her absence and while my father was at work, I babysat my brothers; prepared easy things for their lunches, like SpaghettiOs, Jell-O, and tuna-salad sandwiches; and washed clothes, hung them on the line, brought them in, and ironed, folded, and put them away. My mom paid me five dollars a week for this. This wasn't the first or the last time in which these were the conditions of my summer vacation—my mother gone, me babysitting, my father always remote or irritated with me, it seemed. But for some reason during the summer following my sophomore year, I felt abandoned and that I was being punished for wanting my life to be more like those of my friends, who spent their summer days swimming and sunbathing at Lake Geode, thirteen miles west of Burlington, or hanging out with each other downtown or at Crapo Park, a beautiful old park created on a high bluff above the Mississippi, with a fountain, a swimming pool, and a wide view of the river, the bridges, the bluffs, and the floodplain.

That spring, I had received the news that I was accepted into the regional youth symphony orchestra for the summer. I'd dreamed of being part of the symphony ever since it had performed at my middle school, when I was astonished and smitten as the members, kids not much older than I was, played the fourth movement of Brahms's Symphony no. 1 in C Minor. Surely this movement had been greatly shortened and heavily arranged for high school students, but even so, when I heard Jane Madden play the piercing flute solo, I was enraptured. I yearned to hear that beautiful, plaintive melody again so that I could sing and play it myself. But all I knew were the opening notes, which I played over and over. I was thrilled that I, too, would be playing grown-up music at the rehearsals that summer, and I couldn't wait for the first one.

I was an inconsistent student, knocking myself out in history, English, sociology, and psychology, but showing far less motivation in math and science. I wasn't one of the fast-track kids who would win scholarships and awards, but I carried a B+ average and took a mix of regular and college-preparatory classes. My greatest triumphs at school were music-related. In seventh grade, I was last-chair flute in the concert band. Over the summer, I practiced like mad. At the auditions at the beginning of eighth grade, Mrs. Juhl, the new band director, herself a flutist, sat me in first chair. When another flutist saw the new lineup with me at the helm, she asked if there had been a mistake. Mrs. Juhl said that this was no mistake: I was the one she'd chosen to be section leader. The summer after eighth grade, I began flute lessons with Mrs. Juhl in her home. For years, I had also been playing, partly by ear, partly by reading music, an old, out-of-tune upright piano that my folks bought at an auction for ten dollars. That same summer, Great-Aunt Pertsie bought me a brand new spinet piano and I started lessons with Mrs. Bailey. I had great ambitions and advanced quickly. I wanted to be a concert pianist and marry Van Cliburn, and I wanted to go to Interlochen Summer Camp and even sent away for an application, though when I saw how much money it cost, I never filled it out.

Playing in the youth symphony seemed to be an important step toward achieving my musical goals. But with my father at work at the railroad and my mother far away during the summer of '72, I had no transportation to the rehearsals. It didn't occur to me or anyone else at my house that I might be able to take the bus or get a ride with someone else in the symphony. Nor could I imagine using my bicycle for anything other than leisurely rides to Crapo Park and back or to Mrs. Bailey's house, which was just a few miles away from my house. I was more angry than sad when I had to tell the director's assistant that I couldn't come to the rehearsals and I wouldn't be performing with the symphony at the middle schools or anywhere else.

To say that I began dieting in response to these circumstances is to attribute more intention and deliberation to that act than I remember being there. By some bizarre logic, I seem to have felt that because I was deprived of my mother and the chance to do what other kids my age were doing, I should also deprive myself of food. I cannot say if at that time I saw this as self-punishment or as a protest that I hoped would draw the attention of others to something that needed to be righted. What is true, though, is that I ate less and differently. In the beginning of that summer, for breakfast I ate two Pop-Tarts. The rest of the day, I ate fruits and vegetables. And for the first time in my life, I ate my meals alone.

Like many of my friends, I'd signed up to take driver's education during summer school. I didn't know how I would get to the high school on the other side of town once or twice a day without someone to drive me. But I was determined to complete the class so I could get my license when I turned sixteen in September. Great-Aunt Pertsie took off from the rubber factory in Keokuk and stayed with us during the first week of summer school. I don't remember whose idea this was. Though we saw her regularly and she was devoted to us, she never spent the night at our house, so it was remarkable that she stayed several in a row. She drove me to and from the simulations, driving practices, and early morning classes at the high school. And she bought me Pop-Tarts and fruit.

When Great-Aunt Pertsie returned to work, I was on my own again. I had to find some way to get myself to the high school and back. About this time, something clicked, caught, or shifted deep in my brain and effortlessly, overnight, it seemed, my relationship to food changed utterly. I, who had never had the willpower to diet for more than a few minutes, suddenly felt empowered to deny my appetite, and in turn, I was empowered by this denial. It was a click that I heard and a shift that I felt as I slid into a different gear. I may not have been conscious of this at the time, but because I heard the click and felt the shift again when I was twenty-five and fifty-four, the other two occasions when eating very little became so easy and gratifying for me, I suspect that it happened that first time, too. Without the shift, dieting requires teeth-gnashing willpower. But in that other, higher gear, dieting is a piece of cake—or when dieting is agonizing, it's also bearable because it's so exhilarating and fortifying. After the shift, I dropped the Pop-Tarts and ate no more than six hundred calories a day, mostly cantaloupe, lettuce, broccoli, cabbage, tomatoes, peaches, puffed-rice cereal (not with milk, but dry, as one would eat popcorn), an occasional hard-boiled egg, and lots of diet pop. I consulted the calorie counter in my mother's cookbook until I'd committed the amounts and totals to memory: "Lettuce, 1/5 large head, 10 calories"; "Cantaloupe, 1/2 5-inch melon, 35 calories." I don't know where I got the idea that six hundred calories was ideal, though perhaps it had something to do with the fact that I've always liked the number 6. Now I suspect that I was actually consuming far fewer than six hundred calories per day. After all, how much lettuce and how many plums can one girl eat in a day? I took great pleasure that summer in baking cookies, cakes, and brownies for my brothers and my dad but never eating any of it myself, never breaking my faithful, rigid adherence to my daily calorie limit—except for once. One morning when I was making chocolate chip cookies, I took a tiny taste of the dough. It was so creamy, so sweet and salty, and the hard little chocolate chips so tasty. I ate another dab of dough, promising to skip lunch and dinner in exchange. But suddenly, a wall tumbled down and I wolfed big gobs of the dough. I couldn't stop until over half of the double batch of dough was gone. I felt tormented with guilt afterward and frightened by the knowledge that my unruly appetite wasn't gone or diminished, as I had thought. Rather, it was there and, because of the harsh denial, more out of control than ever. I put the lid back on and gave it an extra hard, wrenching turn to the right.

What astonished me that summer wasn't how little I ate but how much I had consumed before the shift. I was also amazed by what a clever, creative dieter I became. I discovered that if I craved a tasty, high-calorie snack—cookies, doughnuts, catsupy meatloaf, Rice-A-Roni, Doritos tortilla chips—I could take one mouthful after another, chew it well, enjoying the flavors and textures, and then just spit it out: I got most of the pleasure with none of the calories. But on this diet, bread was verboten, so I never ate it, nor did I ever chew and spit it. Even then, I knew that bread was my binge food, which means that, except when I'm in a very healthy mode, I either gorge on or abstain from it. All or nothing. I chose nothing. This was unfortunate since industrial white bread (sixty calories per slice) is fortified with iron, which might have prevented the anemia that left me so weak that about a month into my diet, I could barely pedal my bicycle to the high school and back.

Within eight weeks of severely restricting my caloric intake, my saddlebags were gone. According to the 1959 Metropolitan Life height/weight table that I found in one of our cookbooks, a small-framed, five-foot two-inch female who weighed what I did was average or normal. (According to the 1983 revision of this table, I was slightly underweight at the end of the Punishing Summer.) I was finally normal, except that I'd stopped menstruating, my hair was falling out, I smelled bad because I was burning fat instead of carbohydrates, I was so anemic that no matter how long I'd slept I awakened deep-down tired and weak, I thought about food constantly, and I had frequent nightmares in which I caught myself eating pizza or glazed doughnuts. But I didn't mind since I relished the sense of mastery and accomplishment I found in becoming smaller and smaller. And, too, I had a sense that some error or flaw was being corrected or erased and that some greater reward was being prepared for me, though I couldn't imagine what either was. Dieting hurt so good.

Other than at driver's education, which I took with my friend Holly, I didn't see any of my friends that summer, not even my friends next door, Ellen Lloyd and her sisters, whom I'd hear talking and laughing on their front porch. Some evenings, I heard male voices mingled with theirs. Rather, I stayed home and did laundry and dishes, practiced my flute, baby-sat, rode my bike, exercised along with *The Jack LaLanne Show,* watched programs that featured skinny women like Cher and Barbara Eden, read paperback novels by Ayn Rand, Leon Uris, Graham Greene, Jacqueline Susann, and others, and waited for my next precisely measured and calorie-calculated meal. I was a bookish, introverted kid who didn't mind being alone. But that summer I was lonely. Even so, it was more important that I punish myself for something I couldn't identify and my friends for not appreciating me enough. When they saw how much weight I'd lost, they'd realize how much time had passed since they'd last seen me and feel really bad. I'd accept their apologies, though not immediately. They'd have to wait, worry, and beg a bit.

My isolation gave me plenty of time to daydream about walking into the band room once school started in low-slung, hip-hugging, bell-bottom blue jeans and a tank top. I would look so good that every drummer and trumpet player in the band would gawk at me as they elbowed their stand partners, and the girls would gasp and exclaim. But for every daydream I had about wowing people with my trimmer body, I also had one about starving my worthless self in order to get even—though I never fully fleshed out the "why" or the "with whom."

I was angry with my mother. When she came home on the weekends, I did my best to ignore her. Abstaining from interacting wasn't so different from abstaining from food. When she came home at the end of the summer, I was still mad and kept snubbing her for a while. But, too, I was relieved, so very, very relieved, that she was back and that I didn't have to bear responsibility for so much. My mother took me to see the pediatrician, mostly because I was worried about my hair loss. Also, I wondered why I hadn't had a menstrual period since I started dieting. The doctor didn't use the terms *anorexia nervosa* or *eating disorder*. His specialty was allergies and allergy-related asthma in children, so he may not have known about this disorder. But even if he did, he might not have seen my symptoms as those of a discrete disorder since neither the first nor the second edition of the *Diagnostic and Statistical Manual of Mental Disorders* (*DSM*), published by the American Psychiatric Association in 1952 and 1968, respectively, offered a description of or criteria for diagnosing anorexia nervosa. It wasn't until 1980, eight years after the onset of my malady, that the third edition of the *DSM* provided the following diagnostic criteria for the disorder:

A. Refusal to maintain body weight over a minimal normal weight for age and height, e.g., weight loss leading to maintenance of body weight 15% below that expected; or failure to make expected weight gain during period of growth, leading to body weight 15% below that expected.

B. Intense fear of gaining weight or becoming fat, even though underweight.

C. Disturbance in the way in which one's body weight, size, or shape is experienced, e.g., the person claims to "feel fat" even when emaciated, believes that one area of the body is "too fat" even when obviously underweight.

D. In females, absence of at least three consecutive menstrual cycles when otherwise expected to occur (primary or secondary amenorrhea).

Even though I'd lost 22 percent of my body weight in just a few months, I still weighed enough that I met only three of the four standards. Later editions of the *DSM* modified the weight requirement, and the *DSM-5*, published in 2013, changed the criterion to one that is more open ended: "a significantly low body weight in the context of age, sex, developmental trajectory, and physical health." That, I met.

Now I wonder how the idea came to me, a rather isolated teenager in a small town in Iowa in the early 1970s, that self-starvation was a solution to those problems of mine that seemed so overwhelming and insurmountable. It wasn't through direct transmission since I had never heard of anyone who self-starved or chewed and spit, much less known anyone who'd done those things, though I had certainly known many people, including my mother and my maternal grandmother, who crash dieted for short periods of time and then gained back the weight they'd lost and sometimes more. During one of her diets, I remember my mother declaring with triumph and defiance, "I'm hungry and it feels good."

So how *did* I—three years before that shocking article "The Self-Starvers" was published in *Time* magazine, eleven years before Karen Carpenter's death made *anorexia nervosa* and *bulimia nervosa* household words, a decade and a half before the surge of confessional memoirs and TV talk-show guests broke the silence about what were long considered if not taboo, at least private matters about women's bodies, and several decades before the glut of "pro-ana" (pro-anorexia) websites began portraying self-starvation as a glamorous lifestyle choice rather than the deadliest of the psychiatric disorders—develop such disordered-eating behaviors? And why did my expression of my malady vary so little from everyone else's? Now "wannarexics" or "wanna-be anas," those who don't have anorexia but claim to or pretend to because they want to lose weight and feel special, can learn the symptoms of anorexia through websites, books, magazines, and movies. But I had none of that. My almost textbook symptoms simply appeared.

Chewing and spitting, a behavior that I confess here for the first time, is one that for forty-some years I thought of as mine alone. Because I was convinced of the uniqueness of this behavior, I was ashamed by my wasteful refusal to swallow perfectly good food and of the masticated globs that I hid at the bottom of the kitchen garbage can or spit into the toilet. But while doing research for this book, I learned that this form of purging behavior is common among those with eating disorders and disordered-eating behaviors. Common! Is knowledge of such behaviors carried in the air like unseen *Mycobacterium tuberculosis,* which causes tuberculosis outbreaks? Is it instinctive, like eating clay when iron deficient? Do eating disorders and disordered eating spur creativity and inventiveness, each case inventing itself in a unique yet similar way? Or are the symptoms entirely predictable, like the excessive thirst and urination of diabetics or the tremors and the stooped, shuffling gait of those with Parkinson's disease?

After the doctor examined me, he said that my condition was similar to the malnourishment seen in European concentration camps during World War II. I remembered photographs of skeletally thin people whose ribs were so prominent that you could count each one, whose knees looked enormous because the flesh on the thighs and calves was gone, and whose eyes stared at the photographer out of dark pits. I don't remember him asking me what I'd been thinking when I so drastically cut my food intake. Nor do I remember him ordering a complete blood count or checking my serum iron level. I suspect that he saw me as just a silly teenaged girl who was overzealous in her dieting. My doctor said that the solution to my hair loss and amenorrhea was simply to eat more—which is like telling a depressive to cheer up or a diabetic to make more insulin. And yet, I did start eating more. The day after my mother returned to us, she and my father went grocery shopping and returned with a bag of glazed doughnuts. I sat at the dining room table and devoured three. They were delicious. Then I returned to my restricting. A few days later, my mother bought lunch at McDonald's and took my brothers and me to Perkins Park for a picnic. It was the first time I'd ever eaten a Big Mac, and I loved it: the triple sesame bun, the cheese, lettuce, pickles, and Thousand Island-like sauce, and the thin hamburgers. I believe it was during that meal that I clicked and shifted out of the gear that had made starvation, isolation, and epic bike rides easy. The suddenness and ease of this change perplexes me. The easiest explanation is that my malady had been a simple hunger strike. When my mother returned home and fed me, my demands had been met and I ended my protest. But eating disorders and disordered eating aren't simple or easily explained, and usually not easily "cured." I now know that they are the result of a complicated stew comprising genetics, brain chemistry, and familial and cultural influences. In truth, my malady had been stewing for a long time before I manifested symptoms.

This time, I regretted the click and the shift because once I was no longer in that higher gear, dieting was almost impossible. And as my malady loosened its grip on me, it also released its embrace: I would miss terribly the power and intensity and euphoria of its hold on me during that long summer. Never again would eating be an innocent act, undertaken simply because my body needed nourishment.

CHAPTER TWO

WHITE BREAD

The white bread that I grew up on was an industrial marvel. It was pure, uniform, convenient, had a soft, minimal crust and a long shelf life, and was cheap. As is often the case, people didn't know they wanted these things until they got them.

Eighty miles north of Burlington, in Davenport, Iowa, Otto Frederick Rohwedder, a jeweler, invented the Rohwedder Bread Slicer in 1912. It seemed like a good idea, yet all the bakers to whom he showed his invention rejected it since sliced bread quickly dries out and grows stale. Rohwedder tried holding the slices together with long hat pins, but the pins wouldn't stay in place. The solution, he realized, was to create a machine that both sliced the loaf and wrapped it in plastic. Finally, in 1928, Rohwedder found a baker, Frank Bench of the Chillicothe Baking Company, who was willing to give the multi-knifed bread slicer a try. Sliced Kleen Maid Bread went on the store shelves in Chillicothe, Missouri, on July 7, 1928. "So neat and precise are the slices," the *Chillicothe Constitution-Tribune* reported the next day, "and so definitely better than anyone could possibly slice by hand with a bread knife that one realizes instantly that here is a refinement that will receive a hearty and permanent welcome." The electric pop-up toaster, which appeared at the same time, made uniformly sliced bread a new necessity. Two years later, Wonder Bread of Indianapolis began offering pre-sliced, plastic-wrapped loaves.

But freshness and predictability weren't enough. People also wanted their uniformly sliced bread to have tiny, even cells instead of the irregularly sized gas-bubble holes found in homemade bread, some of which can be so big that the grape jelly or yellow mustard falls through onto your lap and stains your clothes. "Continuous mixing," a process developed in the United States in 1953, involved batter-whipping, which sped up the process and offered the desired fine, tight grain.

In Mrs. Nye's ninth-grade foods class, I'd learned the traditional sequential process of bread making: mixing the ingredients, then kneading, then letting the dough ferment, then shaping, then baking the entire batch of dough. But with the "continuous mixing" method, a consistent and uniform stream of dough meant that all these stages were happening at once, so dough could be worked from the time the ingredients were mixed until the dough was placed in the pans, without the usual interruptions while the yeast worked. This eliminated the long waits followed by bursts of activity to shape and bake the loaves. Manufacturers appreciated the speed of the process and the uniformity of the result. Consumers appreciated that the bread looked and tasted better. An early television commercial for Wonder Bread declared that "because Wonder soft-whipped bread is made from batter not dough, it has no holes." By the mid-1970s, this rapid-production method accounted for 60 percent of all commercial bread produced in the United States.

In the 1960s, among Americans in the counterculture—student radicals, hippies, war protestors, and other dissenters—white bread became a symbol of all that was corrupt and vapid about the dominant mainstream culture. Theodore Roszak, in his 1969 best seller *The Making of a Counter Culture: Reflections on the Technocratic Society and Its Youthful Opposition,* said that white bread was the perfect metaphor for the reign of technocrats and "capitalist desperados" who, for the sake of efficiency, reform, and modernization, robbed us of our imagination, our emotionality, and our individual freedoms. "Not only do they provide bread aplenty, but the bread is soft as floss; it takes no effort to chew, and yet it is vitamin-enriched," Roszak wrote. Consequently, the foods one chose to eat or not eat became a means of taking a political stand. More recently, in "Revolution in a Can: Food, Class, and Radicalism in the Minnesota Co-op Wars of the 1970s," Mary Rizzo noted, "If America's technological superiority and wealth was symbolized by finely milled, mass-produced Wonder Bread, then eating coarse, homemade dark bread was a simple but powerful way for the counter culture to make a statement against the prepackaged, rationalized consumerism of Cold War America by return-ing symbolically to a simpler and purer era before industrialization and capitalism."

During my growing-up years, in the late fifties, the sixties, and the early seventies, white bread was what we toasted for breakfast, ate as the foun-dation of a bologna and catsup sandwich for lunch, or spread with butter or margarine as a side dish with our supper. On rare occasions I was of-fered other types of bread, like Mrs. Lloyd's homemade white bread or the store-bought rye that my mother used when she made Reuben sandwiches, which were new and all the rage in the early 1970s in Burlington. But white bread was what we nearly always ate, and the phrase "so white bread" was how culturally and politically sophisticated people might have described the place and the people I came from—white, middle-class, middle-America people, people as seemingly bland and generic as bread made with flour from which the color, texture, and nutrients have been ground and bleached. By refusing to eat industrial white bread, I had found—albeit unconsciously—a small but symbolic way of setting myself apart from the people and the place I came from.

I was born on September 4, 1956, during some of the darkest days of the Cold War, when the number one song in the country was Doris Day's "Que Sera, Sera (Whatever Will Be, Will Be)" and the number one television program was *I Love Lucy*, to a family in Burlington, Iowa. The population of Burlington, a beautiful old railroad town on the Mississippi, peaked at 32,430 in 1960 due to the demand for nuclear and conventional weapons produced at the Iowa Army Ammunition Plant in nearby Middletown.

During my childhood, Burlington was a booming industrial town. Al-most anyone could get hired at the J. I. Case Company, General Electric, Exide Technologies, Champion Spark Plug Company, the Winegard Com-pany, Murray Iron Works, the Burlington Northern Railroad, or the Iowa Army Ammunition Plant. What they manufactured, backhoes, switch-gears, batteries, spark plugs, antennae, turbomachinery, locomotives, and weapons, were practical items that made other industries possible. A pair of factory workers could earn enough money to buy a nice house, put two cars in the garage, take their annual family vacation to Disneyland (or, in the case of my family, a week-long fishing excursion to Leech Lake in northern Minnesota), and send the kids to college.

My family consisted of my parents, who remained married even though they didn't get along or seem to like each other very much; two brothers, Jamie, who is two and a half years younger than me, and John, who is almost nine years younger; three grandparents, who lived nearby and were a steady presence in our lives; an uncle and his wife, whom we seldom saw; and several great-aunts, one of whom, Great-Aunt Pertsie, was especially dear to me. To my great regret, I had no sisters or cousins.

When I was in elementary school, Jamie and I went to Sunday school and Bible school and received pins for good Sunday school attendance every year at our Methodist church. My family went to church more for the social events than for the religious and spiritual offerings. But I loved all of it—from the potluck dinners, ice cream socials, and talent shows, to the Sunday school classes, where we read Bible stories and learned about John and Charles Wesley, the founders of Methodism, to the songs we sang, "Holy, Holy, Holy," "Trust and Obey," and "Open My Eyes that I May See." When I was in seventh grade, we stopped going to Sunday school, though we still occasionally attended worship services.

My father was a boilermaker, first for the Chicago, Burlington & Quincy Railroad and then, after the merger of the CB&Q and several other railways, the Burlington Northern. My mother was a secretary who went to college when I was in upper elementary school. Upon graduation, she was hired to teach biology at the high school, which substantially increased our financial well-being. We lived in a gracious California bungalow on Main Street, midway between downtown and Crapo Park. We had two cars, orthodontics for my brothers, and flute and piano lessons for me. My parents worked hard, bowled in a league, and ate dinner at the Eagles Club some Friday evenings.

Of course, the times in which I grew up were extraordinary. When I entered Corse Elementary School, the teachers and the principal could spank children and lead them in the recitation of the Lord's Prayer. School prayer was outlawed in 1962. But corporal punishment persisted. When I was in third grade, a substitute teacher hit some kids on the backs of their hands with a ruler during math and the principal paddled those boys who were particularly tough cases. When I was in fifth grade, I was assigned to the classroom of Mrs. Helen Berry, a new hire and our district's first black teacher. When I entered eighth grade, the district switched from the junior high to the middle school model and the school board approved a proposal that allowed girls to wear pants to school. When I entered high school, I didn't go to the three-story brick-and-limestone building atop West Hill, with tall windows in every classroom and a panoramic view of downtown, the school that my father had attended, but a brand new, dull, tan box with window-less classrooms in a field on the west side of town. When I was in high school, the Kresge store on Jefferson Street closed and Kmart, another brand new, dull, tan box, opened in a field on the west side of the city. How had we ever lived without such low prices for so much stuff that we really didn't need? The times, they were a-changin'.

Even as a child, I yearned to be something other than "white bread"— bland, typical, unremarkable, working hard for a paycheck, living for the weekend, ending up at Aspen Grove Cemetery. Some kids had labels that identified them as different—Polish (an unusual ethnicity in my home-town, where most of us were of British, Irish, German, or Scandinavian descent), Jewish (only a handful lived in Burlington), farm kids (at the be-ginning of each school year, the school secretary came to the classroom to count and record their presence), military kids who lived in government housing at the Iowa Army Ammunition Plant (they, too, were counted). Some people came from other parts of the country, places with histories that gave them identity—the Civil War and slavery in the South; colonial-ism and the Revolutionary War in the Northeast; cowboys, Indians, and battles over natural resources in the West. But the Midwest, my part of the country, didn't have a grand, central narrative.

I wanted to be unique, distinctive, someone you'd pay attention to. But I was nothing. Actually, I *was* something: I was a pudgy, dorky kid with more B's than A's on my report card and sometimes, a few C's. In high school, I could have been identified as a band nerd, except that I hadn't yet encountered that term. Once I told my father that I wanted to go to a different church. "Like what?" he asked. I was stumped. The only church whose name I knew was the one we attended.

My desire to be something other than white bread is one of the reasons why my preferred babysitting customers were a couple of Jewish families who had moved to Burlington from other parts of the country. I don't know which I found more exotic, that my worldly employers were affiliat-ed with Temple Israel, a small building with overgrown shrubs and a Star of David on the side and that held services one Friday evening per month, or that they sometimes said things like, "When we lived in California . . . " or "When we lived in Chicago . . . "

My desire to be something other than white bread may also have been the reason why during my junior year of high school, the year that followed the Punishing Summer, I hung out with Alphonso. "Alfie," a relay runner on the track team, was tall, slender, and black, wore an Afro, and walked on his toes with a bounce, as if he were ready to take off sprinting at the sound of the starting gun. My friend Ellen hung out with his twin, Augustus, "Augie." Alfie wasn't a love interest of mine, though we sometimes held hands and once, we kissed. Because their father, an officer in the army, had been transferred from Texas to fill an administrative position at the Iowa Army Ammunition Plant, Alfie and Augie lived in government housing on the base. When the Atomic Energy Commission phased out nuclear products at the plant a couple of years later, Alfie's family would return to Texas. Because Alfie was black and came from far away, he offered a double antidote to my white-bread life. My father and his mother were staunchly opposed to this friendship because Alfie was black. Because of my alliance with Alfie, Grandma Knopp even referred to me as "Liza Jane." My mother didn't seem to mind, though I thought it best not to tell her family that I had a friend who was black. Once, on our way from the military base in Middletown to my house in Burlington, Alfie had to stop at the truck stop. I loved and hated that when we walked in, all the old coffee-drinking guys stopped talking and stared at us as if we were freaks. At that exhilarating and frightening moment, I was not white bread.

Because Dad was a railroader, he had an Amrail Travel Privilege card, a free pass for the entire family on the newly created Amtrak. The fall following the Punishing Summer, my mother, my brothers, and I, or sometimes just my mother and I, would ride the California Zephyr into Chicago, that wild and alluring city, on a Saturday morning, shop and eat, and then ride the train home that evening. I loved watching the scenery become less rural, less residential, more concentrated, more urban as the train carried me across cropland, through the western suburbs, and into the city and to Union Station. In Burlington, our tallest building was the eight-story Farmers & Merchants Bank & Trust, but the buildings in Chicago really did scrape the sky and block the sun. I was dazzled by the sheer number of people in downtown Chicago, some of whom spoke languages other than English; I loved the food (oh! the Italian Village) and the clothing choices, the likes of which I'd never seen in Burlington; and I was impressed that the city had a rock band (Chicago) and a soul group (the Chi-Lites) named after it. I didn't fully comprehend how incredibly uncool and behind the times the folks in my hometown and I were until I started going to Chicago. For instance, I viewed the Academy Awards as previews of those movies that might be coming to our theaters. But those movies had already played in the theaters of Chicago. Our day trips to Chi-town, as I sometimes called that wonderful city, intensified my desire to be someone other than who I was and to be somewhere other than Burlington. I listened to *The Larry Lujack Show* on WLS, 890 on the AM dial, broadcast from the Loop in downtown Chicago. I felt urban and "in the know" as I followed the rush-hour reports as to whether the traffic on the inbound Eisenhower or Stevenson was stalled or flowing freely. I felt hip as I sang along with the songs from the WLS Hit Parade any time of day—something one couldn't do with KBUR, Burlington's old-fogey station, since the hits on it were confined to a top-ten *hour* on Sunday evening, followed by Billy Graham's *Hour of Decision.*

I saved the money I earned babysitting so that on my trips to Chicago I could buy unique clothes at the Marshall Field's or Carson Pirie Scott bargain basements. Blue suede platform oxfords. High-waisted, cuffed, blue-and-white plaid pants. Short-sleeved, waist-length cardigans. Cuffed, pink hot pants. A short, navy-blue knit dress with an embroidered yoke and ties in the back. In my Chi-town threads, I was not white bread.

My mother, Granny Parris, my dad's aunt Flossie, and I were bookworms. I read just about everything, from the popular fiction and mildly trashy paperback novels that Granny devoured during the night shift at the hospital nursery where she worked (Leon Uris's *Exodus,* Jacqueline Susann's *Once Is Not Enough,* Ira Levin's *Rosemary's Baby,* and anything by Erskine Caldwell, Pearl S. Buck, Ayn Rand, or James Michener) to the hardback novels and nonfiction from the Book-of-the-Month Club to which Great-Aunt Flossie had belonged since World War II (my favorites included Benedict and Nancy Freedman's *Mrs. Mike,* anything by John Steinbeck, and a biography about Simon Wiesenthal, the fierce Nazi hunter). Most important, though, were the books that I picked out for myself at the Burlington Public Library, where members of my family had been borrowing books since the red sandstone building perched near the top of North Hill opened in

1898. I fell in love with Melanie in Margaret Mitchell's *Gone with the Wind*, Huw in Richard Llewellyn's *How Green Was My Valley*, and Cassandra in Dodie Smith's *I Capture the Castle*.

I used to believe that I always had my nose in a book to fill time and empty spaces during a summer vacation or even a weekend that yawned deep, wide, and long before me. But I now believe that I was such an ardent, ravenous reader because the exotic people I met in the books I read—like Kira Argounova in Ayn Rand's *We the Living*, who not only wanted love and romance but a profession, that of an engineer; or the audacious, real-life Isadora Duncan, who danced barefoot simply because she wanted to; or Juliet Capulet, who broke family rules to marry Romeo—were people who caused things to happen rather than waiting around for things to happen, as I did. Sometimes, I met kindred spirits in books, like the gawky social misfit Frankie Addams, who was unbearably bored and restless with her life and her hometown in Carson McCullers's *Member of the Wedding*. I was forever hooked on the opening lines: "It happened that green and crazy summer when Frankie was twelve years old. This was the summer when for a long time she had not been a member. She belonged to no club and was a member of nothing in the world. Frankie had become an unjoined person who hung around in doorways, and she was afraid." Frankie's desperate, misguided efforts to find a place where she can fit in are tragic and comic. Yet eventually, she comes to terms with herself, finds people with whom she can belong, and reaches a truce with the conventional.

I also read because I wanted to be a writer. In fifth and sixth grades, I had written two novels, *A Ballerina You Shall Be* and *Scotland Calls*, in six-by-nine-inch, lined Stuart Hall tablets, and in the summer following seventh grade, I'd written and illustrated a poem about a different flower each day in a spiral notebook. I liked this work and wanted to be rich, famous, and admired for it. The writers whose biographies I knew fell into one of two groups, which offered me a troubling choice: one group included men who lived large and answered their appetites—Truman Capote, an affected and often audacious guest on the *Johnny Carson Show*, which I sometimes watched; Ernest Hemingway, who shot himself in the head rather than live a diminished life; and John Steinbeck, who traveled with the Okies to California, to the Sea of Cortez to collect invertebrates with the biologist Ed Ricketts, to the Soviet Union with a photographer, and all around the United States with a big blue French poodle named Charley. The other group of writers included Emily Dickinson, Charlotte Bronte, and Louisa May Alcott, introverted spinsters who stayed too close to home for my tastes.

My first understanding of my malady was that it was an act of passive rebellion. It's not uncommon for a child to use food as a form of rebellion by refusing to eat what everyone else does, which often means that the parents, or, most often, the mother, prepare one meal for the family and Campbell's Chicken & Stars soup or a grilled-cheese sandwich with the crusts trimmed away for the "finicky" kid. Certainly, I was protesting the conditions that I found so oppressive the summer following my sophomore year. But, too, I may have been protesting the idea that my appetites were supposed to be satisfied by a menu and schedule that someone else had determined (as a child, I couldn't go out to play until I'd finished my salmon patty or minute steak or creamed, canned peas). Or perhaps I was protesting the white-bread lifestyle and values that I found stifling. I had long desired to be something other than uniform, predictable, denatured, and relatively tasteless white bread. What I hungered for was meaning and authenticity, but I knew on some level that what we in middle America were being fed—philosophical materialism and a version of Christianity from which the mystery, passion, and revolution had been drained—couldn't nourish us. Now I wonder if I rebelled by glutting myself with soft, batter-whipped white bread, the only bread I knew as a child, believing that if I ate enough, I would get full. Once I realized that there was no way that industrial white bread, devoid of nutrition and fiber, could ever nourish or satisfy me, I rejected it. "That's soooo white bread" became the worst thing I could say about any belief or situation.

Now I wonder why I spurned the conformity, the conventionality, and the typical standards of success that so many others either accepted or embraced. As a teenager, I loved rebels—Janis Joplin, who instead of listening to Bobby Darin and Connie Francis as a teenager listened to Bessie Smith, Odetta, and Big Mama Thornton; Joan Baez, who was frequently sent to jail for protesting the Vietnam War; Jean Seberg, the actress from Iowa who had played Joan of Arc and was at one time rumored to be pregnant with the child of a Black Panther (a rumor started by the FBI in response to her work with the NAACP and the Black Panthers' free breakfast program); and the Irish hunger strikers, even though I didn't understand what they were objecting to. Yet my favorite television program was *The Waltons,* which debuted just weeks after the Punishing Summer. It offered a solidly patriarchal home, conventional male-female relationships, and children who, beyond a little surface opposition, were essentially obedient, something middle America seemed to crave in response to a public that was divided about the validity of our involvement in the Vietnam War and the long labors and hard, messy births of the various social-equality movements of the 1960s. I was envious of the Waltons, who prayed together and shared the news of the day as they sat elbow to elbow on benches at a long table, where they ate hearty, homemade meals—pork chops and milk gravy, baking powder biscuits, eggs on hash, corn on the cob, and lots of cobblers and pies. There was no catering to picky eaters in that family! Because of their orderly, disciplined yet nurturing home life, when the Walton children left their big, harmonious family for jobs, marriage, or military service in far-flung places, they were never unmoored and set adrift. I was drawn to Olivia's wise, maternal presence and to her loving marriage. But, too, I was drawn to John Boy's writerly sensibilities. In fact, I wanted to be both a wife and mother and a writer . . . if such a thing were possible.

Then, I didn't know that there were alternatives to pre-sliced, plastic-wrapped industrial white bread. I didn't know what different types of bread there are in the world—whole wheat, sourdough, cornmeal and molasses Anadama, buckwheat barley, spelt, bagels, pita, potato, and rye (Lithuanian, caraway, pumpernickel). Then, I didn't know that there were alternatives to the white-bread version of the American Dream, which involved automatic dishwashers, houses where every child had his or her own bedroom, and color televisions numbing the mind with *The Price Is Right* or *Hawaii Five-0* or *The Waltons,* all paid for with secretarial or assembly-line jobs at the factory that manufactured the antennae for televisions or the explosive components for nuclear bombs. I couldn't see that my growing-up place was distinctive; that there were people there who sought to restore the American Dream to its original vision (described as "not a dream of motor cars and high wages merely" but one in which every person is "able to grow to fullest development" by James Truslow Adams, the historian who coined the term *American Dream* in 1931), and that one day, I'd be deeply grateful for having grown up on that bend in the Mississippi River and among the people of my hometown. Then, I couldn't imagine that as an adult, I'd keep returning to my growing-up place physically and in my thoughts, my dreams, and my writing. Then, I couldn't yet imagine the various ways in which I, just a chubby, dorky, above-average, white, middle-class, Protestant kid from Burlington, Iowa, could counter the effects of white bread.

CHAPTER THREE

OTHER KITCHENS, OTHER TABLES

When I entered my junior year of high school, I had a new look. Instead of covering myself with roomy pullovers, I tucked in my shirt to show off my lean form. Just before school started, I went to Younkers and bought a pair of trim blue jeans and a white and turquoise, gingham-checked polo shirt. I remember them because the jeans were size 5 and the shirt was a Small. Once again, my gym suit had room to spare. My old, size 11 jeans, which I'd worn before my weight loss, hemmed so they fit my short, stout frame, hung in my closet, too big to be taken in. New clothes were expensive, so my mother sewed skirts for me, some of which were only slightly longer than my blond hair, which almost touched my thighs. When my tenth-grade history teacher saw me walk past her classroom, she ran out the door into the hall in the middle of class and called to me. "You look terrific!" she said as she looked me over. "How did you do it?"

"Eating less," I said as if it were the easiest thing in the world to do. "Just six hundred calories a day." She wrinkled her brow in response.

With the exception of my bread binges, I ate normally before the Punishing Summer, though just a little too much of everything—two pieces of pie when one should have been enough. After the Punishing Summer, I was either stuffed or starving all the time. I was consumed with thoughts of food and weight, ran a daily calorie total either in my head or on paper, and stripped down and weighed myself several times a day. If I gained weight or consumed too many calories, I was anxious and angry with myself. Even then, I knew that my preoccupation with food wasn't normal. Even then, I knew that the severe restricting that had followed the click and the shift had tinkered with something essential, a mechanism or the default settings in my body or brain, or both, that had been responsible for turning on and shutting off my appetite. Just as a child or puppy deprived of love spends the rest of its life seeking the attention it lacked, my self-imposed starvation created a hunger that I feared could never be satisfied. Thereafter, eating or not eating was a more conscious and intellectual decision than one based in hunger or satiety.

At school, I no longer bought hot lunches with the combinations that I loved—like chipped beef and milk gravy on mashed potatoes, buttered corn, apple crisp, and a puffy white roll with a pat of butter—because they were too fattening. Instead, I'd buy a couple of apples from the a la carte line. During the first semester of my senior year, I ate lunch in the cafeteria just once. The rest of the time, I spent my lunch period in the library with my buddy from Algebra III, Denise, a tall, slender girl who was always dieting. As we solved polynomial equations, our stomachs rolled with hunger. When I arrived home from school, I headed straight for the kitchen. I was so ravenous by then that I ate whatever I could find—leftover fried chicken, scalloped potatoes, dressing and gravy, hamburger patties, slabs of cake, wedges of my mother's excellent pie, and white bread, two slices at a time—while standing at the refrigerator, counter, or sink. Then I was full. Really full. Too full to join my family for dinner. Which was fine with me. Too often, my parents were at odds with each other, which made family dinners tense and unpleasant. I was glad to have a reason to retreat into my bedroom and read or practice my flute or listen to the hits on WLS.

One day when Denise was gone, I went to the cafeteria and joined up with Mary Pelzer, a girl I knew from Sunday school. As we chatted, she got in line for a hot-lunch tray. I hadn't had one since I was a plump, girdle-wearing sophomore. The food looked and smelled delicious. Mary said that she had to eat a big lunch because she went to work at the Hy-Vee grocery store directly from school. It would be a long time before she would eat supper. Food was fuel and fuel was energy, and energy was what she needed for a long day of school and work. Even then I envied Mary's honest, practical approach to food. I bought a tray, too, and ate the food with relish—all of it. Afterward, I used the Dell Purse Book *Count Your Calories,* which I carried with me, to calculate the damage. A sloppy joe sandwich, 415 calories. Tater tots, 160. Catsup, 20. Fruit cocktail, 97. Chocolate cake, 235. Milk, 166. Had I really put away 1,093 calories at one meal? I kept retallying the calories. Surely there was some mistake. I was filled with guilt and disgust and couldn't concentrate on my schoolwork the rest of the afternoon. Curiously, I didn't see coming home from school and scooping cold, leftover chili or macaroni and cheese into my mouth with Doritos as I stood at the refrigerator as a problem. That was supper, and I'd be full from it all evening. But this was early in the day and I'd be hungry again by evening. And, too, lunch in the school cafeteria was public eating and couldn't offer the soothing release of rhythmic, trancelike, private eating.

In spite of my constant attention to the scale and to my caloric intake, I couldn't moderate my eating. Many weekends, I dieted—limiting myself not to 600 calories, but to 1,000 or 1,200 calories a day of regular food, usually English muffins, eggs, and vegetables, and six cans of diet pop, followed by an evening jog down Barrett Street and back. When on Monday morning I weighed a pound or two less than I had the preceding Friday, I felt triumphant. Then I returned to my unregulated eating. I was sentimental about the Punishing Summer. Not that I wanted to be in charge of the household from the time I got up until my father returned home from work or have to bike everywhere or be so alone, but the mastery and order I'd achieved then was an enviable thing. I yearned to return to that state of mind in which not eating or eating very little had been so easy. But try as I might, I couldn't find the path, the door, the key, the way back in.

I recognized others who had belonged to the same "club" as me. Jane Madden, who had played the Brahms flute solo with the youth symphony, lost over twenty-five pounds at the same time that I did. Jane lived in what seemed like a mansion to me. She wore monogrammed cardigan sweaters and wool skirts and pants to school, which I guessed that she'd bought at J. S. Schramm Company, a department store in downtown Burlington that had the most expensive, elegant, trendiest clothes in town. I couldn't afford to buy any of the clothes at Schramm's, even those on the end-of-the-season sale rack, but Grandma Knopp bought me something nice and practical at Schramm's every Christmas, like a white blouse or a plaid wool skirt. Once I saw Jane at King's Food Host. Her friends were eating cheese frenchees, onion rings, hamburgers, and milk shakes, but Jane had only a tall glass of iced tea that she sipped through a straw.

Nickie Morano was also in the club. I didn't know her, but I heard rumors that she had lost so much weight so fast that the doctor told her she'd never be able to have kids. Sue Gilbert was in the club, too. She and I didn't know each other since we weren't in the same classes. But my friend Cathy Wurtzl knew her, so one time when Cathy and I were on our way to a high school baseball game, we stopped by Sue's house, an old farmhouse on the outskirts of town. As the half dozen or so kids that Sue was babysitting ran around the yard, she explained that she had lost gobs of weight by eating only once a day and then, only cereal and milk. Once a day! I would perish. I liked my six hundred-calorie-a-day weight-loss program better: six tiny meals per day comprised of low-cal fruits and vegetables. But Sue's diet was working. During her punishing summer, she lost so much weight that she had to borrow a belt from her dad that she cinched tightly to hold up her faded, baggy jeans.

Adults were in the club, too. One of the women whose kids I babysat was thin, glamorous, and always dieting. She even had a scale for weighing food on her kitchen counter. Mrs. Rich, my ninth-grade health and physical education teacher, was also one of us. On the day in my ninth-grade Foods I class that we fried doughnuts, Mrs. Rich stopped by the classroom to see what smelled so good. As she watched us eat our freshly glazed doughnuts, she told us that she had just lost nineteen pounds on a lettuce and water diet. Then, I couldn't imagine enduring such austerities. Yet I didn't find what she was doing abnormal. Mrs. Rich was plump, and she was doing something about it. That was good. After the Punishing Summer, I remembered how exhilarating it was to take control of one's messy life by watching the numbers on the scale become smaller and smaller, so I envied those who were deep into their diets or diseases.

The boys noticed my new appearance. But I was so self-conscious that I tended not to notice their attention until someone else pointed it out to me. And then I didn't know what to do with it. The summer following my junior year, Cathy and I went to Steamboat Days, Burlington's annual riverfront festival. I wore the cuffed, pink hot pants and platform sandals that I'd bought in Chicago. As we strolled through the midway, even I was aware of the looks that I received from both the hometown guys and the carnies. The next day, Jay Jamison, a tough farm kid who went to a rural high school across the river in Illinois, rode a motorcycle, and sported a long scar on his left cheek, telephoned me. "I seen you at Steamboat Days," he said when he called. He said that he had asked around to find out which

Knopp my dad was in the phone book. For our first date, we saw the James Bond movie *Live and Let Die,* which I found about as interesting as the Watergate hearings. Though we continued seeing each other, we never went anyplace again since Jay preferred hanging around my house, watching TV, and making out on the sun porch.

Jay was handsome and alluring in a bad-boy, rebel-without-a-cause way, but I never felt at ease with him. He liked to talk about all the thin, pretty, popular girls that he'd dated at my high school, and he was far more sexually experienced than I was, which made me feel shy, awkward, and lacking. The second time we made out, he stuck my hand down his pants. "Just put it in your mouth," he whispered urgently. I obeyed, but had no idea why he'd want me to do such a bizarre thing. But he did. In fact, we had to do this every time he visited. Once, Jay went to Chicago with my mother and me. For a special treat, we stayed overnight in an old railroad hotel. Mom and I shared a room, and Jay had one to himself. After we returned from dinner, I went to Jay's room to watch television with him. We almost had intercourse, which I knew far more about than fellatio since I read pulpy novels and several times had read parts of a book that I found in my mother's bookcase, Harland William Long's *Sane Sex Life, Sane Sex Living: Some Things That All Sane People Ought to Know about Sex Nature and Sex Functioning; Its Place in the Economy of Life, Its Proper Training and Righteous Exercise,* published in 1919. But just moments before penetration, I told Jay to stop because I was afraid of getting pregnant. And he did.

After our return to Burlington, I heard nothing from Jay, which I found odd after having spent two full days together and almost going "all the way." I felt sick to my stomach. Soon, I was doubled over with jabbing pains in my abdomen. The doctor said that I probably had an ovarian cyst that had ruptured and admitted me to the hospital for observation. While I lay in the hospital bed, woozy from the painkillers, I wondered why Jay wasn't calling or visiting. Hadn't I done almost everything he had asked me to? He was going to feel really rotten when he learned that I'd been hospitalized and he hadn't visited. I had a dim awareness that the pain in my stomach was more closely linked with what had almost happened with Jay in the hotel room and his subsequent and complete disappearance from my life than anything to do with one of my ovaries. This may have been the first time that I perceived a link between my emotions and my body. I spent one night in the hospital. When I went home the next day, the doctor told me to simply watch the matter and see if it happened again. The jabbing pain in the lower left side of my abdomen didn't return, but my body would continue to speak to me about what I was ignoring, sometimes with a whisper, sometimes with a shout or a shriek.

When I returned to school as a senior, my experience with Jay left me feeling worldlier, yet also even more perplexed about males. But my confusion would soon dissipate. Early in my senior year, Ellen and I and two new friends, Monty and Ben, were driving in Crapo Park late one Friday night. I sat in the back with Ben. He was my age but a year behind me in school. He had a blond, Beatles mop-top haircut, bright brown eyes, and a short, taut gymnast's body. I found him absolutely adorable. And he was a nice guy. As we listened to Mick Jagger's plaintive "Angie," a song about the end of a romance, Ben's hand inched across the backseat until it touched mine. My stomach flipped with delight. A few minutes later, Monty, who was driving too fast on the curve near the ball diamonds, slammed into a telephone pole. Ellen took a bite out of the dashboard that undid several hundred dollars' worth of orthodontics. Because of the conniving and collaboration involved in developing a story that would keep us from getting in trouble with our parents, the police, and Monty's insurance company, we all got to know each other pretty well. Soon, Ben and I were going steady.

Ben lived with his dad and brothers in a duplex. He was on his own, coming and going as he pleased, doing homework or cleaning his room only when he wanted to. He had to pay for everything he needed—clothes, gas, car insurance, and school lunches. When we met, he was working three jobs, at a grocery store, a gas station, and the YMCA, where he taught gymnastics. But when he got more hours at the gas station, he dropped the other two jobs and worked only there, every weekday afternoon from four to six and Saturdays from eight to six. Every evening after work, he came to my house. We did homework together, watched TV, and after my parents went to bed, had sex. He was my first serious boyfriend, my first love, the first person I'd had *real* sex with (oh, how he made me bloom like an iris on a warm spring day)—the kind of sex that made me feel bold and beautiful, the kind that felt good. Ben and I treated each other well and planned to be together always. He would become an architect; I would become a concert pianist. We'd live someplace other than Burlington, though neither of us imagined where, and we'd name our first son Amos. Ben didn't seem to mind that my weight was inching up until the saddlebags were back and I had to buy bigger jeans.

A couple of weeks before my eighteenth birthday, I left home for the University of Iowa. I had dreamed about and planned for this day for years, but when it arrived, all I could think of was Ben, whom I couldn't bear to leave, so I said I wanted to stay home. My mother, who was not persuaded by my plan to stay in Burlington, continue to work at the florist and greenhouse, my summer job, and marry Ben, drove me to the university, where I moved into the same dormitory that she had lived in during the Punishing Summer. Every weekend, I went home to be with Ben. In October, he broke up with me, saying that he found the long-distance relationship just too difficult.

Surely, I could change his mind. I went home the following weekend and asked Ben if we could talk. He said that he'd stop by in the evening. I spent the afternoon curling my long hair, applying makeup, dressing in my best Chicago threads, and dabbing myself with the Tigress perfume that Ben's aunt had given me for Christmas. I looked and smelled great. But Ben was firm: we were done; he'd moved on. I was hurt and bewildered. What about our plans? What about all that time we'd spent together? Did all men leave as easily as Jay and Ben?

I wish that I could report that after my heartbreak, I devoted myself to my music. But I didn't. I thought that being a music major would be a continuation of what I had done in high school. But it wasn't fun, like playing flute in the BHS band and orchestra, where I was first chair. The summer before I left for college, Mrs. Juhl and I had worked on a sonata by Francis Poulenc and a Mozart flute concerto. She thought I was terrific. But at the university, my flute professor, a former metallurgist with NASA turned flute expert, assigned me nothing more difficult than easy scales and simple exercises as we focused on my embouchure, breath control, and tone development, with the promise that the following semester, we'd play simple baroque suites. My piano teacher, a mercurial Italian from California, said that my playing reminded him of the cows in the Iowa countryside, placidly chewing their cud. "Where's the passion? Where's the fire?" he asked, his dark eyes blazing and his hands waving. I didn't understand the concepts in Music Theory. I appeared to be tone deaf in Aural Skills. Everyone in concert band was so much better than I was. As my social life grew busier, I found it harder and harder to do the minimum required practice, two hours for flute, two hours for piano, each day.

During the four semesters that music was my declared major, I was an utterly lackluster student. My shortcoming was a lack of discipline, which posed greater problems with each passing semester. I didn't want to study or practice. Instead, I wanted to go on dates, go to parties, stay out late, and sleep in. During my freshman year, I dated Don, a fashionable guy who was from Iowa but had lived in California for a few years before returning home. Don liked his women very thin, so I dieted and worked very hard in Figure Control, one of my physical education classes. Over the noon hour, five days a week, the other women in the class and I did butt lifts, saddlebag lifts, squat thrusts, toe touches, windmills, and lots of sit-ups as our stern teacher with the steely thighs and calves counted our repetitions. The goal wasn't losing weight but gaining control and tightening up—something that I knew could be more easily achieved with a girdle. Nonetheless, I gritted my teeth, flexed my muscles, and completed all the reps. At the end of the class, I was firmer and more flexible and very, very glad that the class was done. With what little money I had, I bought new, smaller jeans. Still, Don would berate me if in the dormitory cafeteria I chose something really yummy, like a piece of coconut cream pie, even if the only other food on my tray was rabbit food. It never occurred to me to tell Don to worry about what was on his own plate instead of mine or to get up and leave the table when he started picking at me and sit with people talking about more interesting matters—like Monty Python, the fall of Saigon, or the guy in our dorm who'd been lured away from classes and keggers by the Jesus Freaks. Don left me for Jackie, who kept herself model-thin by throwing up most of what she ate. A few years later, Jackie and I would live and work together.

My lack of discipline was a problem with food, too. I absolutely loved dorm food. With so many dishes to choose from, I rarely ate meat and didn't miss it. I enjoyed the salad bar every lunch and dinner, both the standard fixings for a chef salad and some of the weirder combinations, like creamy coleslaw with Spanish peanuts. I had never seen yogurt before; I ate it at every meal. I loved the ice cream machine. I loved pancakes or waffles for breakfast. I passed on the white bread, preferring "brown" bread, which was exactly like industrial white bread in shape and uniformity but was tan. I'd eat two pieces of bread with the meal and take two pieces with me, which I would eat as soon as I got back to my dorm room. I tried to pace myself so that I could eat three meals a day in the cafeteria, but it was so easy to pack in all my allotted calories for the day at one meal—a version of the Sue Gilbert diet—then have to starve the rest of the day. Or I would succumb and eat even more. Once again, I was soft and unruly.

In 1973, the year before I entered college, the Iowa legislature lowered the state's legal drinking age to eighteen, a grave mistake that it corrected five years later by raising the legal drinking age to nineteen and in 1986 to twenty-one. But when I entered college, eighteen-year-olds could buy alcohol anywhere. Every dorm refrigerator held a bottle or two of Boone's Farm apple wine or a six-pack of Budweiser. Instead of going to wholesome dorm parties, my friends and I went to keggers in dorm rooms or apartments, or we went to the downtown bars, where we danced and drank whiskey and water. Just as I had in high school, I kept gaining and losing the same pounds, over and over again. But when under the influence of alcohol, my eating was even more out of control. After we closed the bars, we'd head to our favorite greasy spoon, Hamburg Inn, for omelets or tenderloins and hash browns or to the dorm vending machines for corn chips and mini doughnuts. During my sophomore year, I started smoking Marlboro Lights in hopes of controlling my weight and to look a little cooler when I was out on the town. When I first started smoking, I felt woozy and nauseous and lost a few pounds. But soon, I had a two-pack-a-day habit, my appetite had returned with gusto, and I couldn't climb a hill or play my flute without getting winded.

The summers following my freshman and sophomore years, I moved back home, where my life seemed drab and restrictive compared to my life in Iowa City. Everyone I'd been close to in high school was gone or married, so I had no one to run around with. Nor would I have had the time since both summers, I worked at the Burlington Care Center, a nursing home in Crapo Park, where I was the head breakfast cook. I'd clock in no later than 5:00 a.m. and start boiling water so I could have a vat of oatmeal, ninety poached eggs, an urn of coffee, and a big jar of iced tea ready by 6:30, when the nurses' aides came to pick up the breakfast trays. Every other Sunday, I was the relief lunch cook, preparing and serving the same meal: baked ham and canned pineapple, canned sweet potatoes and marshmallows, canned green beans, and poke cakes made from white cake mixes and red or green Jell-O. The rest of the time, I did prep work, like picking the cooked meat off chicken bones or making stacks of sandwiches (peanut butter mixed with an equal amount of margarine on white bread; chicken salad that was mostly Miracle Whip) or washing dishes. My greatest responsibility was correctly filling the trays for bed-bound residents according to dietary specifications: bland, sugarless, low-calorie meals for those with diabetes; bland, low-sodium meals for those with hypertension; bland, soft meals for those with dental or digestive problems; bland, low-fat meals for those with heart problems; bland, liquid diets for the very ill or dying. Some residents had several of these problems and were limited to some tasteless pap like steamed hamburger, pureed carrots, and sugar-free applesauce. One morning, I accidentally scorched the oatmeal. If I had to make a new pot of oatmeal, breakfast would be late and I'd be in trouble, so I sent the burnt gruel out on the trays. I hoped that no one would notice. After all, every morning most of the oatmeal was returned to the kitchen, where we dumped it down the disposal. Only one aide complained about my carelessness. How awful it would be, I thought, to have no control over what you ate or the quality of your food. I nibbled food as I prepared it and drank lots of pineapple juice. By the end of the summer, my white, homemade polyester uniform was very stained and very tight.

During my junior year, I shared an apartment with two Greek-American women, Claudia and Marina, both of whom had won their hometown beauty pageants and gone on to compete in the Miss Iowa contest, with Claudia placing as the second runner-up. They possessed much that I lacked: sophistication, social confidence, beauty, buxomness, ethnicity, and spending money. Claudia, who always seemed to be dieting and working out, taught me how to apply makeup so that my eyes looked brighter and more almond shaped, my cheekbones and jawline more prominent, and my lips fuller. She taught me to pad my bras and tease my hair to give it height and fullness. She encouraged me to take out a bank loan and inject some life into my limited, low-cost wardrobe (I didn't do this). But in the meantime, she'd occasionally loan me clothes from her vast wardrobe, which packed her half of the closet and part of mine. After Claudia's makeovers, I was struck by one of two thoughts as I looked in the mirror: "Who on earth is that person looking back at me?" or "Wow! I look like _____: (a) a country western singer; (b) a disco queen; (c) one of Charlie's angels." But what had I expected? Claudia starred in a car commercial on TV in which she wore a swimsuit and tossed a beach ball. Her ambitions were to marry well, be a devastatingly beautiful businesswoman, and live in some posh and exclusive suburb of Des Moines or Miami. In her, I saw a more costly and refined version of the white-bread lifestyle that I was seeking to escape. And yet, I envied Claudia. She had a dashing, gallant, and utterly devoted Brazilian American boyfriend, and she turned heads wherever she went.

To help pay my living expenses, I worked at a Robin Hood–themed restaurant in the mall where the employees could eat, at no charge, hamburgers, tenderloins, or fried-fish sandwiches and french fries. We could also help ourselves to salads slathered with dressing and topped with homemade, butter-saturated croutons and chopped hard-boiled eggs and the heartiest soups that I've ever eaten—cream of bacon, beer cheese, New England clam chowder. At my apartment, I ate cheap, college-student food—American cheese, bologna, fried egg, or peanut butter sandwiches on store-bought white bread. Sometimes I just ate the bread. Sometimes I stopped at a downtown bakery and bought a half dozen raspberry danishes. I intended to make them last, but as long as there was one left in the bag, I couldn't think of anything else, and ate them all by day's end. My weight soared. It was the most that I would ever weigh, including during either of my pregnancies. One of the few photographs that I have of myself from that time period shows Theresa, my best friend and fellow waitress, and me leaning against the fence that marked off the south side of my dad's vegetable garden. I am short and squat, with thick thighs. The tip of my long blond ponytail is even with my trademark saddlebags, which are loaded with provisions. My upper arms are beefy. I was unhappy about my size, envied thinner women, and only looked in a full-length mirror when I had to, but as much as I wanted to, I couldn't shift back into that state of easy denial.

After my demise as a music major, I had to figure out where I belonged in academia. No matter what was going on in my life, I read. That was constant. Off and on since I was in fifth grade, I had written stories, poems, novels, and once, a play. I switched my major to English, where I could read to my heart's content. I didn't have to go across campus to a practice room in the music building, but could read anywhere—in bed, on the bus, at Hamburg Inn, on break at work between the lunch and dinner shifts at the restaurant. I loved the reading lists for courses such as Introduction to Critical Theory, where I encountered Jane Austen and James Joyce for the first time, and Hardy and Lawrence, where we plowed through a hefty stack of novels. The best class of all, a survey of American novels written since the Second World War, included E. L. Doctorow, Jack Kerouac, Joseph Heller, John Barth, J. D. Salinger, Kurt Vonnegut, Robert Penn Warren, and others. The lectures and class discussions tapped into the deep story about our post–World War II American culture—idealism and cynicism, conformity and experimentation, moral confusion and clarity, and various responses to the American Dream. In that class, I encountered authors and characters who were engaged in a valiant battle with "white bread." Unfortunately, none of them were women. But the writers I met in Women Poets of the Sixties and Seventies—Adrienne Rich, Denise Levertov, Sylvia Plath, Marge Piercy, Mona Van Duyn, and Anne Sexton—offered a far wider range of writerly female role models than the secluded spinsters I'd come across as a child.

Even though I loved literature and writing, my lack of discipline was a problem in my new major, too. I read everything I was assigned, but I had a hard time going to classes, especially if I'd worked the night before at the restaurant and gone out afterward with my coworkers. Keeping up on test preparation and paper writing was also challenging. One day an official letter from the university arrived, informing me that I'd been placed on academic probation and would remain there until I pulled up my grades. Unfortunately, this designation did nothing to inspire better attendance and work habits.

To say that I quit school is to attribute more intentionality to it than it merits. I simply went to class less and less until finally, I wasn't going at all. I spent more time working and hanging out after hours with the crew from the restaurant, which was easy to do since I'd moved into a big house that I shared with four other women, three of whom I worked with, and the boyfriends of two of the women. Jackie, the woman Don started seeing after he dumped me, kept herself whisper thin by vomiting after she ate and snorting the cocaine that Kevin, her drug-dealing boyfriend and our fellow housemate, provided her. Trying to benefit from Jackie's example, I'd stick my finger down my throat after I ate, wiggle it, and cough and gag and spit a bit, but because I had a very weak gag reflex, I seldom vomited. Trying to empty my stomach not only was exhausting but often triggered an asthma attack. At five feet two inches, I was size-13 fat and believed that nothing short of a miracle could change that.

By the end of 1978, I was adrift. I'd been out of school for seven months and several of my friends had moved on to other jobs or cities, so I returned to my parents' home and took a job bartending at a little blue- and pink-collar tavern, a for-the-time-being situation. I planned to save most of each paycheck until I had enough money that I could move to a great city where interesting people lived. But my first car, a secondhand, 1970 green Camaro, which I bought a few months into my job, gobbled up most of each paycheck. Even though I worked full time, I couldn't afford an apartment in Burlington, much less Boston or Minneapolis.

After several months of working until midnight or two in the morning and sleeping until the early afternoon, I enrolled in a journalism class during the summer session at Iowa Wesleyan College, a Methodist college twenty-five miles northwest of Burlington. For my big project, I collaborated with the only other student in the class, a farmer who wrote for a tractor-pull magazine, on a newsletter dedicated to the Equal Rights Amendment, which we both hoped would be ratified into law. I was so glad to be back in school and to have more important things to think about than what to do when I got off work (go home and watch an HBO movie? go across the river to drink at one of the after-hours bars in Gulfport, Illinois?) that I overprepared for everything in this class. On the columns that I contributed to our ERA newsletter, which I typed on a manual typewriter, I justified the right-hand margin—measuring, typing, and retyping until everything was perfect. "Wow," my coeditor said when she saw my straight-edged columns. Hers had ragged right-hand margins. "That must have taken you forever." Certainly, justifying the margins took longer than writing the column. But I so badly wanted to do well. At that moment, I saw how weird and obsessive my ruler-straight columns looked. We received an A on our project, and I received an A for the course. I felt redeemed and believed that maybe if I returned to school, I could be successful.

I enrolled at Iowa Wesleyan for the fall semester. If I could survive four packed semesters, one of which would be my student teaching, and a summer session, I could graduate before turning twenty-five with a BA in English and be certified to teach in a middle or high school. I wasn't sure that I wanted to teach, but I was convinced that I didn't want to be waiting tables or tending bar when I was in my forties like some of my coworkers at the restaurant in Iowa City and the bar in Burlington.

I had tried to fight white bread, mostly by drinking, dabbling with drugs, sleeping around with a diverse assortment of men, each one a little more counterculture than the last, and reading books that challenged the values of the dominant culture. I had tried to fight white bread by not preparing for a conventional occupation like nursing or teaching, which meant that I wasn't preparing for any occupation. I was trying to construct an authentic, independent life for myself, yet there I was living in my parents' home, attending my mother's alma mater—a Methodist College that mostly served students from the surrounding area, a school so tiny that it had fewer students than the elementary school I'd attended—and preparing to enter the same profession as her. Because I was a commuter and had to rush back to Burlington for my evening bartending job the moment classes ended, I wasn't part of the campus life at Wesleyan. In so many ways, I'd settled for white bread.

Even so, I worked incredibly hard. The two science lab classes, both required for graduation, tested my endurance and commitment, and I wasn't terribly fond of the education courses. But I was hungry for the stories and ideas I encountered in literature, history, and educational psychology classes. I did more than was expected of me in each class (except for botany and zoology) and made the dean's list every semester. I student taught at James Madison Middle School in Burlington, which had changed little in the decade that had passed since I was an eighth grader there. It was a little weird eating lunch in the teachers' lounge with some of my former teachers, but it was also satisfying and affirming since they all said that they'd always known I'd make something of myself and were pleased that I'd chosen education for my profession. I was pleased, too. Sometimes when I was teaching and connecting with students, I felt a buzz, a high, a joy.

I rarely baked bread then. But over winter break during my junior and senior years at Iowa Wesleyan College, I worked dough, rich with eggs, oil, sugar, nuts, and raisins, into braided wreaths, which I glazed with egg white or drizzled with white icing. I was making Christmas gifts that I could afford, and I was feeding people's bellies and hearts. I feasted on their delight and approval when they opened the gift boxes and saw the golden braids.

In my last year of college, I dated Pete, a counselor and administrator at Wesleyan. He was the first vegetarian I'd met, and he dismissed heavily processed "food" as almost inedible. Even though Pete had grown up on a farm in western Iowa, he ate foods that I'd never seen the likes of: curried brown rice and lentil stew with mozzarella cheese cut from a brick instead of shaken from a bag; rough granola, to which he added raisins, walnuts, sliced bananas, and milk; dark, grainy loaves of bread that he bought at a natural-foods store, sliced himself, and layered with the kind of peanut butter in which you mix the oil into the solids, raw honey, and sunflower seeds. I had quit smoking just before I met Pete and was enthusiastic about becoming healthier. I adopted his exotic diet as my own.

Equally important, I began thinking differently about food. From Pete's copy of Frances Moore Lappé's *Diet for a Small Planet,* I learned that the solution to the then-looming food crisis was for me to get more of the protein I needed from nonanimal sources and for rich countries like the United States to export grain to starving people instead of feeding it to cattle. From Pete's copy of *Be Here Now,* a guide to Eastern spiritual practices and philosophy written by Ram Dass (formerly Richard Alpert), I learned that what we eat not only affects the functioning of our cells and organs but also "modifies the vibrations of the total organism." The first step in purifying oneself, according to Ram Dass, is to cast off the "habitual meat diet," which I did quite easily. Later, one eliminates those foods that "produce mucus or vibrations which make meditation more difficult." Eventually, the spiritual aspirant finds that fruit and nuts are enough for one leading a contemplative life. Food was fuel, of course, but that it could also be a political statement and a help or hindrance on one's path to enlightenment were new thoughts for me. After just a few weeks on Pete's diet, I lost eight pounds. Thereafter, the pounds came off slowly but steadily. Curiously, I don't remember Pete saying anything, either positive or negative, about my size or my physical appearance.

Pete had thought deeply about American culture and found much that he could not participate in—buying things that you don't need; eating animals or junk food; watching mindless drivel on television; engaging in simplistic, conformity-demanding versions of beautiful, noble religions—in short, going through life half asleep. He practiced yoga, meditation, and mystical Christianity, and scratched away in his journal as a way of gaining insight into himself and his life. "Just because you don't like the answers doesn't mean you should stop asking the questions," Pete often said. Many of my questions were about religion and something that I was encountering for the first time: spirituality. I believed in God and felt rather warmly about Jesus but was barely acquainted with either and never went to church. But after reading several of Pete's books, including Richard Maurice Bucke's *Cosmic Consciousness: A Study in the Evolution of the Human Mind,* Paramhansa Yogananda's *Autobiography of a Yogi,* and Hermann Hesse's *Siddhartha,* I realized that I was far more interested in *experiencing* the divine through meditation and prayer than I was in reading or talking about religion. Within a few months of meeting Pete, I became initiated into Transcendental Meditation, a simple, Westernized meditation technique based on ancient Hindu scriptures; practiced yoga every morning; ate differently and more consciously; kept a journal; and felt guided by something far more expansive, big-hearted, and intelligent than myself—God or Spirit. Perhaps spirituality and healthy, conscious living were the alternatives to white bread I had been craving all along.

Pete's contract with Iowa Wesleyan College wasn't renewed the spring that I graduated, I suppose in part because many nights in a row, my Camaro was parked in front of his duplex just a few blocks from campus. He took a summer teaching position at a small Catholic college in Kansas City and asked me to move with him. We could apply for teaching positions for the fall and settle in the same place, he said. I told Pete that I wasn't ready for such a commitment, but I was grateful for all that he'd exposed me to—different ways of thinking about food, a personal relationship with God, knowledge of how to use writing to gain self-understanding. For the past several years, I'd been lost and estranged from myself, but Pete showed me ways in which I could come home to myself. He continues to be one of the most important influences in my life since everything he introduced me to—spirituality, vegetarianism, yoga, writing, and a skeptical stance toward anything connected with consumerist culture—I continue to practice to this day.

After I graduated, I worked as a bartender at the Eagles Club in Burlington and applied for teaching positions. I baked bread from whole wheat flour and whatever other wholesome ingredients I could find—oats, cornmeal, molasses, and nuts—and filled up on it since it was the most healthful food around. "You made this?" Pete asked approvingly when I brought him a loaf of my round, heavy peasant bread as a parting gift. By the end of the summer, my jeans were loose and I felt both light and full.

CHAPTER FOUR

THE GRAY YEARS

One evening in the summer after I graduated from college, one of the bartenders I often worked with at the Eagles Club in Burlington was drinking at the bar after his shift. He was sitting near the beer taps, so every time I drew a beer, he tried to persuade me to meet him for a little tryst when I got off work. I wasn't interested: he was a dull conversationalist, seemed much older than he actually was, and was married. But we worked together, so I felt that I had to stay on good terms with him. Instead of telling him to buzz off, I was polite but cool.

The club was packed and I was working so hard just to keep up that I didn't have time to eat the supper I'd brought from home or to drink my herbal iced tea, which I'd poured into a Tom Collins glass and set beneath the bar counter. But eventually, I was so hot that I stopped and threw down the tea in a few big swigs. Soon, I felt loose and slightly dizzy: tipsy. How could this be? I had been a weekend drinker throughout most of my undergraduate years and had enjoyed the loosening of restrictions and loss of inhibition that I experienced when drinking, but when I started my student teaching the preceding fall, I had quit—completely. That Pete didn't drink either had made it easy to remain alcohol-free. I was proud of my abstinence since both of my parents drank too much and too often. When I realized that someone had transgressed a boundary and had taken away my choice and autonomy by spiking my drink, I became angry and frightened. I suspected my coworker and confronted him. Yeah, he'd poured a couple of shots of whiskey into my tea, so what? Just relax, enjoy it, and let me know when you're ready for another, he said with a wink.

This seemingly insignificant act set in motion something that confound-ed me and made my life *very difficult*: I developed a paralyzing fear that my food and beverages had been tainted with mind-altering drugs, alcohol, or poison. In addition to this fear, after I ate or drank anything, I felt dizzy and brain-fogged, a state in which my thinking processes were so sluggish that it felt as though I were trying to run through neck-deep water. When I was deep within one of my brain-fog attacks, I felt so swaddled in gray that it was hard for me to follow and participate in conversations and it was a waste of time to try to read since my comprehension and retention were slow and muddy. When I noticed that I wasn't thinking right, I became even more frightened and heedful, watching my thinking, thinking about my thinking, and watching myself think about my thinking. "Lost in the woods" is what I call such loops. In addition to the thought disturbances, there was a distance or barrier between myself and what I was experienc-ing, as if there were layers of gauze or a cloudy film covering everything, blunting my ability to delight in my favorite song playing on the radio, the sunflowers blooming along the road, or the arrival of a letter from a far-away friend. The hazy numbness, lethargy, and detachment that followed my eating a full meal or even a single bite cleared only after enough time had elapsed, usually an hour or two, that I could be sure that my food hadn't been tainted. I find this to be a curious response now since during one of my brain-fog attacks, I experienced the same dulled senses and impaired mental processes that used to accompany my intentional consumption of alcohol, but with none of the mood elevation or loss of inhibition. When I had chosen this state in the past, I had enjoyed it. But at the thought of having it forced upon me, I panicked. If I practiced yoga, the fog burned off a little faster. But sometimes I didn't have the time, energy, or will to wait out the frozen panic or mental paralysis that followed a meal or to perform a series of yoga asanas, so I simply didn't eat.

Initially, I wondered if these symptoms were the result of a physical ail-ment. When my hometown doctor examined me and found nothing amiss, he surmised that low blood pressure might be the culprit and suggested that I start drinking coffee again (because of Pete's salutary influence, I'd given up caffeine and switched to herbal teas). He also gave me little red pills that did nothing to clear my head. Now I wonder if what he prescribed were salt pills, given as much for the placebo effect as to raise my low blood pressure.

During the spring and summer following graduation, I applied for teaching positions. In late July of 1981, I was offered two. One was at a tiny high school in Morning Sun, Iowa, about twenty miles from Burlington. There, I would have been the only English teacher for grades nine through twelve, supervised a study hall, and directed the school musical. The other job was at a large high school in Omaha, where I would be one of about twenty English teachers. I chose the latter because of the more reasonable division of labor and because I was curious about what might be awaiting me in the big city. My mother was away for the entire summer, taking classes at the University of Northern Colorado. We talked often by telephone about my job offers and my upcoming move, but it was Dad who spent a couple of full and frustrating days with me looking for an apartment in Omaha that would take me and my German shepherd, Marta. The only apartments that I could afford and that accepted pets were ones that I didn't consider habitable. I paid a fee at a roommate-locator agency and was led to Stevie, who was a manager in the accounting department at the telephone company. She lived alone with her little dog, Annie, in a three-bedroom split-foyer on a cul-de-sac in a housing development where everyone seemed to be either three or thirty years old and all the trees were little more than saplings. It was soooo white bread, but this was no time for me to be choosy: this was the only decent place I'd found that would take both me and my dog, and I wanted to bring Marta so I'd have someone I loved with me while I was so far away from home. I was desperate to get settled before school started, so I signed a lease and moved into suburbia. My new roommate seemed lonely after her break-up with a married man and she drank a lot. I suspect that she was hoping for someone to cook and eat meals with, to watch television or play cards with in the evenings, and to go out with on weekends. But I wasn't able to provide any of that.

My new job was demanding, and I felt poorly prepared for what was expected of me. I was assigned six sections of sophomore Grammar and Composition and two sections of junior American Literature. While I had a solid background in American literature, I hadn't had a basic grammar course since I was in eighth grade, and I couldn't even identify some parts of speech. Each evening before I did lesson plans, I had to learn the material that I was expected to teach the next day—the use of apostrophes in possessive nouns, for instance, or subject-verb agreement. Though I was more confident about the literature course I taught, I still had much to learn before I could help my students understand the nature of, say, the wild, extravagant optimism that Walt Whitman expressed in *Leaves of Grass*. I found it hard to maintain order in the classroom since I was short, soft-spoken, and, though I had turned twenty-five shortly after starting my new job, didn't look much older than my students. I was shy and self-conscious around most of the other faculty, all of whom seemed to know so much more of their subject matter than I did and were so confident and in charge in their classrooms. I was afraid of the many new things that I had to manage: driving to and from work on a packed interstate in rush-hour traffic; sharing a home with a woman who drank too much; reading and grading written work from each of my 135 students, which was nearly impossible when I was brain fogged, as well as figuring and submitting their quarter grades; locating service providers in my new city, such as a car repairperson and a doctor; and living three hundred miles from the house on the gravel road in southeastern Iowa that I'd shared with my parents, brothers, dogs, cats, horses, geese, and grandparents, who for the past few years had lived in a trailer in the backyard. Everything overwhelmed me. I felt sad and anxious, tender and bruised.

As the semester progressed, my fear and the brain-fog attacks it caused grew more frequent and intense. I believed that carefully controlling what I ate was my only hope to keep myself safe. Never again would anyone take control of my state of mind by poisoning something that I ingested. But all my efforts weren't alleviating my fear or its effects. In response to my escalating anxiety, I developed an elaborate hierarchy of dangerous to safe foods and ate only the safer ones. Dry foods were the safest. Wet foods were the most dangerous, I reasoned, because it was harder to tell by looking at a wet substance whether something had been added to it. There was an entire spectrum in between. An orange, for instance, was more dangerous than an apple because it was softer and juicier. Added to the moisture factor was the access that other people might have had to my food. A jar of strawberry jelly that I'd just opened was relatively safe, even though wet, assuming that the people who made it hadn't adulterated it with drugs or alcohol or some other vague, dangerous substance—a tampering that would have occurred *before* vacuum packing and shrink-wrap banding took place. But an already open jar of jelly in the refrigerator was doubly dangerous since it was wet and open. Someone could have poisoned it after I'd last closed it and I wouldn't have known until it was too late. I was so terrified that alcohol had touched my food and would make me lose control of my mental processes that I didn't want to be around anyone who was drinking because they might spike what I was eating or drinking, as had happened at the Eagles Club, or something could spill onto my food or drink without my knowing it, and increasingly, I even feared that there would be a transference of the state of mind of the one who was inebriated to me. Part of me knew that these thoughts were irrational, crazy even, but I couldn't make them go away. Even being in the same room as drug paraphernalia or unopened bottles of whiskey, wine, or beer, or being in a place where people had been but weren't at the moment drinking or getting high, frightened me. Living with a roommate who drank every evening made home a hazardous, treacherous place.

Eating in a restaurant was especially fraught with danger, so I usually ordered just a plain baked potato when I ate out. If I salted and peppered it (both are very dry), I still worried since many people had easy access to the shakers. If baked potatoes weren't on the menu, I ordered a tossed salad. To slightly lessen the danger of the damp lettuce and juicy tomatoes that might have been touched by many hands during the preparation, I brought my own salad dressing from home. But no matter what I ate (wet or dry, freshly or previously opened, made by my own hands or someone else's) or where (at home, at someone's house, in a restaurant, at work), after I ate, I felt like I was thinking in excruciatingly slow motion. And what I was thinking about was my thinking, watching for glitches and lacunae, watching for evidence that a mind-altering substance was beginning to affect me, fearing that I would lose control of myself, that I would lose myself.

Because of my fear of eating and my dread of the brain fog that followed, I ate less than I was accustomed to. I lost weight steadily. Just a few weeks into the semester, my fear of being tainted became so great that I started eating my meals in my room, storing my food in my clothes closet, and locking my bedroom door when I was away so that my cache was safe from Stevie and her friends. Of course, this created another problem: some foods aren't safe without refrigeration, so I wasted a shameful amount of food, tossing out tubs of warm yogurt, heads of wilted lettuce, bottles of catsup with a bit of a bite because they'd gone bad. Apples were my most reliable food since they kept well without refrigeration and it was obvious if something had punctured the skin because the area turned brown. If eating seemed too risky, I went without. It was easier and far less exhausting to skip a meal than to prepare the food, consume it, and then wait to see if this time, it had happened: I'd been tainted. Once again, I heard the click and felt the shift that moved me into that other, higher gear that was familiar to me from the Punishing Summer. I was restricting again, though not in the same fanatical way that I had that summer. Since I never knew from one day to the next what level of danger I'd find myself in, which determined how much I ate, I can't say how many calories I was consuming each day. I was pleased to see myself getting smaller and weighing less, but that wasn't my chief motive. I just wanted to feel safe, think clearly, and do my job.

As the attacks worsened in severity, I still wondered if my bizarre thoughts and behaviors weren't due to a physical condition. In the middle of the semester, I found a physician and consulted with him about the numbness and befuddlement I felt after eating, though I told him nothing of the fears related to these symptoms. He sent me to an internist at the University of Nebraska Medical Center, who ran tests, including one for my thyroid-hormone function. I was disappointed when the test results came back normal. I was hoping for a condition that could be named and easily fixed. But the doctor said there was nothing physically wrong with me. He didn't even write a prescription for little red pills.

Three months into my lease, Stevie told me that I wasn't working out as a roommate and gave me one month to get out. I hadn't seen this coming. I didn't mind leaving Stevie and I certainly didn't mind leaving white-bread suburbia. But how would I have time during the semester to find an apartment that would take a big, rompy, high-spirited dog and move all my possessions in my Camaro, one trunk- and backseat-load at a time? As it was, I spent most of every weekend on class preparations, grading, laundry, grocery shopping, errands, and bread baking. With great sadness, I returned my dog, my good companion, to my parents, found a studio apartment that, though too far from work, would suffice, and moved. Once I had my own place that I shared with no one, I felt a little safer keeping my food in the refrigerator. Even so, if I learned that a repairperson had stopped by while I was gone or if I forgot to lock my door when I took the garbage out, I'd empty the refrigerator since it was just too risky to chance it. Open food was dangerous since unbeknownst to me, the apartment manager, a neighbor, or a burglar might have come in while I was away and messed with it. Occasionally, I hid food in my closet behind a stack of boxes.

Stevie had never said anything about my weird food-related behaviors and weight loss, though she had suggested that I "find someone to talk to." No one in my family or any of my friends had ever had to "find someone to talk to." When I heard people gossip about someone who'd gone to a therapist or marriage counselor, the subtext in these stories was that anyone who needed such a service had a pretty weak and flawed character. They just needed some self-discipline and a larger perspective. Even so, I knew that something was very wrong with me and that I didn't have anything to lose by talking to a counselor. I found a state agency with a group of therapists in a strip mall not far away. I called for an appointment and was assigned to Karla.

I started seeing Karla once a week. She quickly became a wise guide, soul healer, and mother figure of sorts. I adored her. Often when Karla asked me what I was feeling, I was stumped. "I'm not sure," I'd say apologetically. But with her help, it became easier to locate and articulate my emotional states. At the time, I wouldn't have said that I had a deficit in emotional awareness; rather, I would have said that Karla had a surplus of sensitivity and responsiveness in this area. Once I called her with an emergency: I was so badly fogged in that I felt that I wouldn't be able to go to work the next day and would have to call for a substitute. Since my thinking and responses were so sluggish and there seemed to be a wide distance between what I was experiencing and what I was feeling, even driving through the pea-soup fog seemed risky. Karla made room for me in her schedule, and I drove to see her even though I was afraid to. During our session, she asked me who I was mad at, a question that surprised me. As we went through the possibilities, I realized that I was angry over hurts and denials from long ago. Very angry. Once we'd identified the causes for my anger, I felt unbearably sad. Karla said that I had to allow myself to grieve these losses. During the drive home, I could barely see through my bleary eyes. Once in my apartment, I sobbed deeply, extravagantly until there was nothing left. The fog had burned off. Everything seemed newly born, washed clean, bright, and beautiful. I felt light and hopeful. This was a breakthrough. I came to understand that when I was fogged in, I had to search for the cause of my anger and then coax or drag it out into the light, where I could see it and the sadness it held. Once there, it quickly lost its ferocity and became a squinting, blinking, withering thing.

Now I wonder why or how I attributed to what I ate or drank a condition that was, at least in part, the result of suppressed or denied emotions. Had my personal history, the fact that when I was fifteen, food had been both the problem and the solution, led me to conclude too hastily that my attacks were caused by fear of tainted food? Perhaps if some other unwanted thing had been forced upon me—if, say, someone had broken into my home, or crashed into my car, if I'd been the victim of a medical mistake, if someone had stolen my identity, or if I'd been attacked, like a friend of mine, who, because she was a Good Samaritan and wanted to help, walked out of a restaurant into a fight and received a fist in her face, which led to facial surgery, orthodontia, an addiction to painkillers, and a missed semester of school—my deepest fears and anger would have found a different avenue of expression, a different metaphor. But food is my medium. When life seems particularly threatening and out of control, I turn to food to erect the boundaries I love and crave because they create a strong sense of inside and outside, right and wrong, pure and impure, and because they create the illusion that I am being firmly held in all the right ways. And yet, poisoning and spiking did happen to people, it had happened to me, and it could happen again. Tainted food was both a fact and a metaphor.

After seven months, Karla left for a job as the director of a different agency, which broke my heart. I was certain that I wanted to continue working with a wise woman who could help me understand myself. Each of the therapists I worked with over the next several years was helpful with the challenges I faced: tense family dynamics; anxieties about work and eating; an exciting, spontaneous, and sometimes violent boyfriend; the voice in my head whose sharp self-criticisms I believed. Yet not one of them made any headway with my malady, in part because I was too ashamed to divulge all the details: that I hid food in my closet; that I was afraid that someone had put something on the kitchen counter or on the dishes in the drain rack that would contaminate my food; that if I bought a Snickers bar because it seemed like the safest food to eat when I was hungry and away from home, I couldn't take a bite of it until I'd inspected the wrapper for evidence that it had been pierced by a hypodermic needle; what a terrible dinner guest I was since I asked dozens of questions about the ingredients and preparation of the food being served and then ate barely any of it; how unbearable it was, at times, to be me. Instead, I described my food restrictions as nothing more than a case of rather weird and strenuous dieting.

During my second year at the high school, my job seemed much easier because I was teaching everything for the second or third time. I became friends with Penny and Renae, two new hires, one in English, one in history. Some Saturdays, the three of us would explore a museum, a festival, antique shops, or a historical neighborhood, and we took turns hosting meals for each other in our homes. Though I knew that neither of them would harm me, I was, nonetheless, scared to eat what they served. Partway into each meal, I felt dull and frozen, certain that this time it had really happened and life as I knew it was over. Then I felt that I couldn't follow the conversation or hide my panic, but my friends didn't seem to notice—or if they did, they didn't care. I enjoyed Penny's and Renae's companionship too much not to participate in our group meals, so after I ate their food, or even the food that I'd prepared for them, I would try to clear away the gray as fast as I could. Who are you mad at? I'd ask myself and allow the light and heat of my answer to burn off the fog. Or perhaps a better metaphor is that I'd bushwhack my way as fast as I could through the dark, thick, and tangled understory until I broke into the light and clarity.

In an effort to meet more people, I signed up for a sixteen-week Science of Creative Intelligence (SCI) class that met Sunday afternoons in the home of a teacher of Transcendental Meditation (TM). Ever since I had been initiated into TM when I was with Pete, I had meditated without fail every morning and late afternoon. At the SCI course, we watched drowsy videos of Maharishi Mahesh Yogi droning on in his singsong voice about "the Unified Field of all the Laws of Nature, and the principles by which it governs the coexistence and evolution of all systems in Nature." According to the Maharishi, the transcendence and the deep rest that we partake of through the practice of TM not only bring about an end to individual suffering but create the conditions for world peace. My goals weren't that lofty or selfless. I simply hoped that through the deep rest offered by TM, I'd release some of the stress and anxiety I felt about my job, family, and food. I imagined myself loading up my plate at salad bars with all kinds of wet and mixed-up concoctions or helping myself to the moist glazed doughnuts that my homeroom students took turns providing on Fridays.

If I could resist the urge to take a nap when a video was playing of the Maharishi expounding on some Vedic principle, I often found wisdom in what he said. For instance, the Maharishi claimed that when one's mind is settled and harmonious and one's brain waves "coherent" (a favorite word of his), that affects others in proximity. Conversely, if one is stressed and one's brain waves are "incoherent," that, too, affects others. Of course, what is happening in the consciousness of other people in the room or the arena or the neighborhood affects one in subtle or obvious ways. Lynch mobs. Beatlemania. The outpouring of generosity following a natural disaster. But at the time, I believed that this philosophy of shared consciousness explained, at least in part, my fear of being around people who were drinking or taking drugs since I was sure that their state of mind would affect mine. How much better to be around people who meditated, prayed, or practiced yoga, who were working to reduce their stress, who were working to become more harmonious, peaceful, pure, and coherent.

After we completed the workbook pages over the Maharishi's main ideas at each meeting, we meditated together, an experience that I enjoyed since being in a group in which everyone was producing those slow alpha brain waves was so much more powerful than my individual practice. After SCI class one day, Gerald, one of the other students, struck up a conversation with me. When he asked me for my phone number, I hesitated. I had found his dominance of the discussion irritating and, with his large facial features, his thick waist, and his casual business attire, which I'd discover was what he wore all the time, I didn't find him physically appealing. Yet he was self-confident, almost brash, seemed fast, fun, and mischievous, and had a rich, hearty laugh. What would it hurt if I went out with him a couple of times?

Gerald and I started spending our weekends together. I was glad to have a man to spend time with in the big, strange city. Gerald was no longer, perhaps never had been, a regular meditator, but he wanted to be, which is why he'd come to the SCI class. He believed that if he could tap into that powerful "source of creative intelligence," his restaurant franchise would take off and he'd be the Ray Kroc of barbecue. He hoped that I would help him meditate regularly and improve his diet since he was carrying some extra weight. The latter was a particular challenge. Gerald ate two meals a day in restaurants, one in his own upscale barbecued-rib eatery and one in that of the competition. The rest of the day, he snacked, eating cookies, chips, pistachios. Often, he wanted me to accompany him to restaurants. But when I pulled a little jar of salad dressing out of my purse or became frozen and quiet after I ate, he'd tell me I was absolutely crazy, nuts, bat shit, flipped out, loco. Sometimes he grew testy if I asked the waitress too many questions about the food or if I told her not to cut open the baked potato because I preferred to do that myself—you know, so the potato stays hot.

I continued to have reservations about Gerald. He was spontaneous and impulsive to a fault. He had had lots of women, some of whom called and left messages on his answering machine. Even so, after dating Gerald for several months, I moved from my tiny studio apartment into his spacious apartment, part of the first floor of an old, dark but beautiful mansion that had been built by an Omaha railroad tycoon in 1883. If you had asked me then why I made such a move, I would have answered that though it seemed perilous to keep my food in a kitchen that I shared with Gerald (or anyone else, for that matter), I didn't like living alone in a city where I knew so few people. Besides, Gerald wanted me there.

Since Gerald and I had opposite work schedules, we saw little of each other during the week. But on the weekends, we went to movies, took little road trips, and ate in restaurants. Every now and then, Gerald slipped away to buy marijuana from and spend the night with a woman friend named Bev. Occasionally he threatened me and acted in ways that frightened me; sometimes he hurt me. The worst time was when he threw me on the floor, sat on my chest, wrapped his big hands around my neck, and began choking me. I couldn't breathe, couldn't stop the pressure, couldn't see any way out. What might have been my last thought was that I was going to die right there on the kitchen floor on a late afternoon in June, and my mother would never, ever let this man get away with it. But blessedly, he let go. As my breath and blood moved again, Gerald bit my nose and spit in my face. I can't remember now what we'd been fighting about, but because I felt responsible, at least in part, for what had happened, I didn't call the police or go to the hospital. I was afraid to be around Gerald and also afraid that when I told him that I was moving someplace brighter and safer, he'd become enraged. But instead, he was sweet and repentant. So I stayed a little longer.

I had not planned on getting pregnant. When Gerald told me that he didn't want a child and was willing to pay for the abortion, I realized that I wanted my baby, a little boy that I dreamed about not long after conception, far more than I wanted my baby's father. It also occurred to me that I needed to protect myself and the baby growing within me from a man who had tried to kill me and who slept around. Gerald protested, saying that we should stay together, perhaps even get married, though he didn't seem willing to change his behavior in ways that convinced me of his sincerity. On New Year's Eve, I moved out of his apartment, which made him so angry that he broke my dishes and threw my packed boxes into the yard. At that point, I didn't know that Gerald would choose to have next to no involvement with his son. Nor could I imagine the many repercussions for my son of growing up without a father. I just knew that I wanted to be safe. After I finished the school year in Omaha, I'd move home so my baby and I could be near my family.

I've long thought of my fear of tainted food as an extension of the disordered eating that I had when I was fifteen, and yet, it was also something else. Of course the two episodes were related since both involved seeking control by restricting what I ate. But the motivations were different. During the Gray Years, the paralysis I felt after eating had nothing to do with my weight and everything to do with my denied feelings of anger and sorrow and my fear of being swallowed by some vague force that meant me harm. Some people obsess about germs, or order and symmetry, or their own recurring "bad" thoughts and so perform a neutralizing ritual, washing their hands until their skin is raw, lining things up until they're late for school, work, or life, or repeating a magical, protective phrase until they've atoned for wrong thoughts, while cutting an even deeper rut in their brains with each repetition of the ritual or phrase. But my medium is food, so I kept myself safe by restricting and occasionally binging, by measuring and calculating, by thinking about my thinking after eating, by fretting over purity and safety, by attempting to control others through what I would and would not eat, and by making myself small so that I took up little space. Sometimes this felt like a punishment or a straitjacket; but other times it felt like a firm and protective embrace.

Now I believe that my fears and restrictions in my twenties were due to an anxiety disorder. Now I understand why my therapists offered so little help with my fear of tainted food since I have never, in all my research, learned of anyone else who was afraid that her food might contain a mind-altering substance and so developed the very symptoms she feared upon eating it.

My fear of consuming anything, an unassuming apple, even a glass of water, if I'd turned my back on it long enough for someone to inject or drop something into it (about two seconds), wasn't completely irrational. After all, someone *had* put alcohol in my tea when I wasn't looking. It was possible that what I feared could happen again and in a more damaging form. I remembered the marijuana brownies that some partygoers in my college days ate unaware of the secret ingredient. I remembered the tainted crab meat that my boss knowingly put on the salad bar at the restaurant where I worked in Iowa City ("It'll be good for one more day," he had said as he sniffed the mound of white and red salad, lifted his nose, then sniffed again) and the "stomach flu" that several of our regular customers told us had laid them out later that night. I remembered a story about a boy in Texas who ate a Pixy Stix straw of candy that his father had laced with cyanide in order to collect on the insurance policy he'd bought on his son. To cover his tracks, the father also passed out poisoned Halloween candy to other kids. I remembered the colza oil meant for industrial use but sold as olive oil in Spain in 1981 that killed many hundreds of people and sickened twenty thousand, some chronically. I remembered the Tylenol capsules into which someone had inserted potassium cyanide that killed seven in Chicago in 1982. Not crazy.

My food phobia was also a way of imposing order and control, and of relieving anxiety at a time when my life seemed too hard to manage. I couldn't yet articulate this deep story then. I just knew that I had to be suspicious, I had to be vigilant. The world wasn't a safe place, and no one could be trusted. Or maybe I was the one who couldn't be trusted. What might happen if I was high or drunk or sick? I might lose control—and what would that look like? I'd miss a day or two of work or I'd go to class with nothing prepared and just wing it? I might forget my own routines and do things out of order? Surely bedlam would result. Someone might have to take care of me. Or perhaps I'd become fat and lazy and messy. When I tried to imagine the possible outcomes, I saw only negatives. I couldn't imagine that it might feel terrific just to go with the flow in class discussions instead of following the questions and answers that I'd written out. Or that a spur-of-the-moment road trip to a catfish festival where I would eat a heaping plateful of that tasty, greasy food of my childhood might be just what I needed. *Just relax, enjoy it, and let me know when you're ready for another.* An alluring, seductive, and menacing invitation.

I also sought spiritual answers. I became an ardent student of yoga, attending classes, studying yogic scriptures, and eventually teaching yoga.

I found that discipline appealing because the ancient yogic texts had so much to say about purifying and controlling the body-mind. I started going to church. While I met nice, open-minded folks at a Unitarian church, I needed more of Jesus, so in whatever neighborhood I lived, I found a Lutheran church where the pastor chanted the liturgy and read excerpts from scripture that moved me or a Methodist church where we sang the hymns of my childhood. I yearned to take Communion, but I could only watch as others queued up to participate in the Lord's Supper. Though the wafers that the Lutherans used were thin and dry, they'd been touched by other hands. Though the little glasses of Methodist grape juice and Lutheran wine didn't hold even a mouthful, they were dangerous, triply so in the case of the wine (wet, accessible, and alcoholic). I was an outsider, unable to enter the community or to embrace the metaphors I loved. Why couldn't I partake of the feast, I wondered? Was my faith in God too weak and frail? Was I afraid that I'd get sick and those people in the pews that I didn't know would have to take care of me? That I'd lose control and eat all the wafers or cubes of bread and drink all the wine? That I was too tainted to be deserving of receiving the sacred meal? Or was I afraid that by taking Jesus into my body, someone else would be in control of me? Whatever the cause, each Sunday I went home from church feeling that I'd missed a grand opportunity by not partaking of a morsel of physical and metaphorical bread.

Even so, the worship services were meaningful to me. What I saw in scripture and heard in sermons offered me hope. The psalmist knew how it felt to be lost in the loops of one's own thinking and pleaded for a new perspective: "Lead me to the rock that is higher than I" (Psalms 61:2). The story of the healing of the woman who'd been bleeding for twelve years (Luke 8:42–48) filled me with the certainty that a divine healing for me was just beyond my fingertips. In first-century Palestine, a menstruating woman was considered impure, ceremonially unclean, tainted, as was anyone who touched her or her possessions, which made her an exile among her own people and one who could not hug or even shake hands with another person. The woman had been to various doctors, but none could help her. When she saw Jesus passing through the crowd, she reached out and touched not him but the hem of his garment, and she was instantly healed. At that moment, Jesus felt the power go out of him and into someone else. On a day when he was being jostled by the crowd and touched by so many,

Jesus asked who had touched him—not because he was afraid that he had been rendered ceremonially impure or tainted, but because he wanted to know who out of the many had touched him with such hunger, intentionality, and faith. The once-tainted woman fell at his feet and confessed what she had done and about the healing that had followed. "Daughter, your faith has healed you," Jesus said. "Go in peace." Not only had the bleeding stopped but also she had been granted calmness, tranquility, and freedom. I believed that this could happen to me, too, if only I could reach far enough to touch the hem of the hem.

Also, I created a ritual for myself that had healing, centering aspects. Each Saturday morning when I lived with Stevie, when I lived alone in my first apartment, when I lived with Gerald, and when I lived with my son, I baked bread. Safe, dryish wheat bread made by my own hands and that I could store in my closet without its spoiling. This was the most grounding part of my week. My kitchen felt homey as I mixed and kneaded the dough. While the yeast worked, I waited around, doing little chores—folding laundry, grading quizzes, writing letters. The bread dough was my creation, yet it was independent of me and had a mind of its own, so to speak. Some Saturdays, it took longer to rise than others. Some Saturdays, the loaves were lighter or denser than those of the preceding week. Once I became a mother, I mused over the similarities between baking bread and raising a child. Both required will and surrender; both products were mine and not mine.

When I pulled the bread from the oven, I could honestly say that I had successfully completed a task—something I rarely felt at work, where my days were hectic with class preparations, teaching, grading, bureaucracy, and telephone conferences with parents who didn't seem to care what their sons or daughters were or weren't doing at school, as well as conversations with wonderful students who stopped by for help with an assignment or just to chat. Each morning before I left for work, I sat at the kitchen table and ate thick slices of my homemade bread spread with plain yogurt and drank several cups of black coffee. Two loaves of bread were more than I needed from one Saturday to the next. But after a hard week teaching students how to write "standard pattern essays" or explaining why some people found *The Adventures of Huckleberry Finn* funny, baking bread was what I wanted and needed to do. Curiously, I didn't binge on this bread. I'd eat no more than, say, a fifth of a loaf each morning. Most often I didn't eat again until I came home from work and made myself an early dinner, usually a raw vegetable salad and baked potato. This was my only restricting episode in which I allowed myself to eat bread.

God answered my prayers. When I moved back into my parents' home in Burlington, I was six months pregnant with my son, Ian. Even though both of my parents drank—my mother every day, my father in weekend binges—my fear of tainted food started fading. Perhaps this was because the familiar rules and boundaries, the blessings and trade-offs of living in my parents' home made me feel safer and I was relieved that I no longer had sole responsibility for my baby and myself. Or perhaps as I tried to structure a safe and nurturing environment for my son, I, in turn, felt safer and more in control. When I was hungry, I could talk sense into myself ("Why would anyone here want to hurt me?"), and the waiting period after I ate wasn't as protracted as it had been. I ate in restaurants, ate food from the refrigerator and cupboards, ate the delicious foods that my mother cooked. I'd still feel dull and dizzy afterward, but the bushwhacking was faster and easier in part because I had become better at discerning the denied feelings of anger and sadness that seemed to cause the fogginess. Even so, I gained only about fifteen pounds during my pregnancy. In August, once I was sure that the medical insurance policy that I bought through the school district would cover my prenatal and delivery expenses, I resigned from my job. Though it was hard to give up the freedom and autonomy of living on my own and good medical insurance for my child and me, I was relieved to be at home and with my family, where there were many people—my parents, my grandparents, and Great-Aunt Pertsie—who were eager to love and help with my baby.

Ian was born on August 21, 1984, my parents' thirtieth wedding anniversary. I had a room on the east side of the hospital so I could watch cars crossing the McArthur Bridge over the Mississippi—liquid streams of light. The induced labor had been so long and grueling that I had wanted to cut and run. But my mother and the midwife kept me grounded. My little boy, the one that I'd dreamed about early in my pregnancy, arrived seventeen minutes after midnight. I had a list of possible names for him—Caleb, Jacob, Theo, Benjamin, Dieter, and Ian—but when I saw my son's red hair and blue eyes, I knew he was an Ian. When a nurse brought him to me for his first feeding, I was astonished to see my own eyes looking back at me from his wizened, jaundiced, old man's face. My mother was terribly excited about having a baby in the house, but my father, who seemed to feel that the circumstances surrounding Ian's conception and birth were shameful, had been disturbingly silent on the subject. Yet as soon as he saw Ian, he, too, fell crazy in love with him. On the morning of Ian's birth, Gerald called and sent a dozen red roses, but he didn't visit because he was in California with his new girlfriend. I was both embarrassed by and relieved about his absence.

When Ian was seven days old, I started graduate school at Western Illinois University. On Tuesdays, Ian was in my mother's care; on Thursdays I took him to Tina, whom I had babysat when she was a little girl. On my first commute to the university, I wept during most of the fifty-mile drive about being separated from my baby. Already, I was so deeply in love with him that it frightened me.

The dizzy, drugged grayness that accompanied eating continued fading, decrescendoing, poco a poco. By the time Ian was two, the fear was all but gone. But as my fear of tainted food lessened, my binges returned, though never again with the intensity and frequency of what I'd experienced in my teens and early twenties. Now I wonder about the nature of this healing. Was it that as a mother, I was no longer living just for myself and so didn't have the time, luxury, or desire to be so acutely sensitive to my more fearful inner states? Was it that the ravenous hunger and high caloric demands of lactation so outweighed my fears that I could eat what my body needed and so the healing was primarily biological? Food was fuel, fuel was energy, and energy was what I needed. Was it that I felt safer in the orderly, structured world I was trying to create for my son? Or was my healing of a divine nature and so beyond reason? My weight dropped even lower than where it had been at the end of the Punishing Summer, yet I was eating pizza, cake, macaroni salad thick with Miracle Whip, fried potato cakes, Peanut Butter Captain Crunch cereal, and paired slices of industrial white bread, as well as my regular healthful food—yogurt, tofu, vegetables from my father's garden, and rough hunks of my homemade bread. Whatever the cause, I felt stable and on the outer edge of that wide territory called "normal."

CHAPTER FIVE

NURTURE

When I heard the news of Karen Carpenter's February 4, 1983, death from complications of anorexia, I was neither curious nor empathetic. Though I admired her flawless, velvety contralto, I never cared for her wholesome image and soft-rock love songs with chaste lyrics, more fitting for my grandparents' generation than mine. At the time, I dismissed Carpenter as just another affluent white female with an eating disorder. While her story awakened average Americans to the reality of eating disorders, I was troubled by what the media said about women and girls who had what many magazines and TV anchors called "the slimmer's disease" or what the *People* magazine article about Carpenter's death called the "'good girl's' disease—a compulsive urge to control weight, primarily among female hyper-achievers." Was I, too, just another a "good girl," just another a "hyper-achiever" who sought to control her life through food? And, too, Karen Carpenter was a fool. Couldn't she have proven her point and achieved her goals without dying from anorexia? But when I delved into her story thirty years later, I realized how little free will or agency was involved in her illness and death. I found myself identifying with her hungers, her sadnesses and frustrations, her sense of inadequacy, and her desire to take charge of her life.

The symptoms of Carpenter's anorexia manifested after she went on the then-popular Stillman Diet—high levels of protein, low carbohydrates, eight glasses of water a day—and quickly lost twenty-five pounds from her five-foot four-inch frame when she was seventeen. I can imagine the delight she felt about her slimmer figure and the gratification she found in pleasing her mother, Agnes, whom many portrayed as bossy, overly concerned with appearances, easily stressed, and unable to give her daughter the love and affection she craved. By 1975, when Carpenter was twenty-five, her weight had dropped from 145 to 91 pounds. Her boyfriend, Terry Ellis, cofounder of Chrysalis Records, said that her mother was upset over how thin Karen had become. According to Sherwin Bash, who managed Karen and her brother, Richard, Carpenter liked the attention she was finally receiving from her mother.

What happened to Carpenter as a result of her first diet and subsequent weight loss isn't uncommon. In an article published in *Paediatrics & Child Health,* Sheri Findlay observes that teenage dieting "has been associated with a fivefold to 18-fold increased risk of developing an eating disorder. However, it is unclear whether dieting causes, triggers or represents the first stage (prodrome) to the illness." But clearly, crash dieting is "the usual antecedent" to the onset of anorexia nervosa or bulimia nervosa.

According to the *DSM,* there are two subtypes of anorexia nervosa: the restricting type ("dieting, fasting, or excessive exercise") and the binge-eating and purging type. Carpenter had the latter. Eventually, she became so weak and exhausted from her restricting, binging, and purging that the duo had to cancel performances. In January 1982, she finally admitted she had a problem, took a hotel room in New York City, and began working with Steven Levenkron, a psychotherapist who specialized in treating eating disorders and the author of several books, including *Treating and Overcoming Anorexia Nervosa* and one of the first novels and movies about the disorder, *The Best Little Girl in the World.* When Carpenter entered therapy with Levenkron, he wanted to admit her to an inpatient facility (she weighed seventy-eight pounds), but she refused to go. After many months of therapy, Carpenter was still taking diuretics and laxatives (eighty to ninety tablets of Dulcolax each night), still purging, still excessively exercising, and still weighing in at less than eighty pounds. In September 1982, she agreed to be hospitalized. As an inpatient, she quickly gained thirty pounds through hyperalimentation, an intravenous feeding procedure that was a treatment of last resort. But apparently she wasn't at peace with her fleshier thighs, her fuller face, her life. To speed up her metabolism, she took ten doses per day of Synthyroid, a drug used to treat hypothyroidism (her thyroid was normal), and massive daily doses of ipecac syrup to induce vomiting. On the day she died, she had taken a particularly large dose of the latter. Her potassium levels were so low because of the purging that her heart stopped and she collapsed in her childhood bedroom in her parents' home in Downey, California. Her mother found her and tried to revive her, but Carpenter had slipped into a coma and within the hour was pronounced dead at the hospital. The autopsy report listed the cause of her death as "emetine cardiotoxicity [ipecac poisoning] due to or as a consequence of anorexia nervosa." Levenkron claimed that Carpenter had beaten her anorexia and that it was the laxatives that killed her.

Carpenter's story is important for what it reveals about what many people thought and some continue to think about the cause of anorexia nervosa. Most who speak or write about Carpenter attribute her excessive dieting to one of two factors. One is the idealization by the entertainment and fashion industries of unrealistically thin women. In my research on Carpenter, I have come across numerous references to a *Billboard* magazine review that referred to her as Richard's "chubby" little sister, a review that might be apocryphal since I haven't been able to locate it. Supposedly, such comments pushed Carpenter over the edge into anorexia.

Another widely cited reason for Carpenter's eating disorder is the behavior of her cold, hypercritical mother, whom some describe as a dragon woman, harridan, control freak, and the ultimate stage mom. In a 1996 *New York Times Magazine* feature, Rob Hoerburger summed up Carpenter's angst: "If anorexia has classically been defined as a young woman's struggle for control, then Karen was a prime candidate, for the two things she valued most in the world—her voice and her mother's love—were exclusively the property of her brother Richard. At least she would control the size of her own body." In *Little Girl Blue: The Life of Karen Carpenter*, Randy L. Schmidt presents anecdotes showing Agnes's unabashed favoritism toward Richard and quotes Evelyn Wallace, Agnes's friend and co-worker at North American Aviation, who said, "From the time Karen was little, everything was 'Richard, Richard, Richard.'"

Schmidt says that another contributing factor was the "family's refusal to let her grow up or feel in charge of her own life." Agnes took control of the finances of her celebrity daughter and son; she still gave them allowances as late as 1970, when Karen was twenty and Richard twenty-four. Eventually, Bash convinced the family to hire a professional money manager. When Karen was twenty-four, she wanted to move out of the family home yet was afraid to ask her mother's permission. Instead, she asked Wallace to ask for her. After Wallace posed the question, Agnes telephoned her daughter and told her that she was a traitor. It would be another two years before Carpenter moved into her own apartment.

Another revealing incident occurred in 1980, when Carpenter learned that her fiancé, real estate developer Thomas J. Burris, hadn't told her about the vasectomy that he'd had many years earlier and that they wouldn't be able to have the biological children she desired. Carpenter wanted to call off the wedding, but because so much money had already been spent on the celebration, the invitations had been sent, family was flying in from London, and a crew from *People* magazine was coming to do a story on the wedding, Agnes refused to allow her daughter to back out. The marriage lasted fourteen months. Schmidt reports Bash as saying that he believed Agnes loved her daughter but wasn't able to express it. "I think eventually that was one of the most serious problems that Karen had. . . . Over the years, Karen Carpenter became beloved in the world as a very special artist, a very special voice who reminded everybody of the daughter they wished they had. In her home she never was told or maybe never even felt that existed from her parents, especially her mother."

According to Schmidt, Levenkron said that the entire time Carpenter was in New York City, eleven months, she received no telephone calls from her family—something he'd never seen among those with anorexia that he'd treated. He finally convinced the Carpenter family to attend a ninety-minute counseling session at his office, at which he told them, "I think Karen really needs to hear that you love her." Agnes was not able to do this. "Well, I'm from the north and we just don't do things that way," she said. Levenkron called Agnes an "oppressive-dependent" mother. "At first she appeared to be overbearing but that same domineering presence is often times a cover for her fear of losing her daughter—or at least control over her daughter."

Carpenter's father, Harold, who is portrayed as sweet and submissive, is rarely mentioned in the stories about the familial influences that contributed to his daughter's deadly disease. Schmidt reports Evelyn Wallace as saying, "Many times I wondered how he could live with that woman the way she used to yell and scream at him. She would jump on him, and he would never fight back. He just sat there and took it. He wasn't a sissy but just a real nice guy. Agnes was the speaker, so he wasn't really one to get a word in edgewise." Surely Harold's unwillingness or inability to protect his daughter from her mother was a factor in his daughter's illness.

When a child is physically or mentally ill in a way that can't be easily explained, it's common and easy to blame the mother. Not so long ago, some believed that autism is caused by chilly "refrigerator moms." That attention-deficit/hyperactivity disorder (ADHD) is caused by mothers who can't provide consistent discipline. That "failure to thrive" is caused by mothers who can't accept the mismatch of temperaments between them and their children or who aren't woman enough to produce an adequate supply of breast milk.

I don't remember if I first encountered the idea that my malady was my mother's fault from something a therapist told me or if I absorbed it from popular culture, both from the Karen Carpenter story, as communicated through magazine and television coverage, and from the comments people make when speaking about those with disordered eating or eating disorders ("She's just trying to get Mommy's attention" or "Her mother must've been a real Joan Crawford"). Either way, long before I became a mother and saw for myself how hard it is to do a decent job of parenting a child, I blamed my mother, and my mother alone, for my malady. During the summer of 1972, she went away. I felt that I'd been abandoned, that I was valuable only if I was taking care of others, that there was no one who cared enough to give me what I needed to thrive. In short, that I was unworthy. In the earliest stories I told about my malady, more to myself than to anyone else, my illness was connected not with my father, a dutiful, physically present man who often seemed either annoyed with or disinterested in me, but with my fiercely loving though sometimes physically absent mother. Curiously, it never occurred to me that my father also could have noticed and talked to me about my binging and restricting, my weight loss, anemia, and isolation. But he didn't.

Only recently did I look into the work of Hilde Bruch, a pioneering researcher in the area of eating disorders, obesity, and family dynamics and one of the most prominent voices in our understanding of anorexia nervosa. I found her idea of ineffective mothering as a chief cause of eating disorders strikingly familiar. Theories and philosophies can trickle down, be borne in the air, or be absorbed as if by osmosis, and Bruch's theory, if not her name, is well known by just about anyone with an interest in eating disorders. In spite of the research in the past several decades about the genetic and biological causes of eating disorders, in spite of the depth and breadth of Bruch's descriptive and theoretical model for defining anorexia, the general public still attributes eating disorders to skinny fashion models and bad mothering.

Bruch's early research was endocrinal, which led her to found an outpatient endocrine clinic for obese children at Columbia University's Babies Hospital. In her early research on the obese sons of Italian immigrants, she gathered data that disproved the glandular theory of obesity, the predominant paradigm in the 1940s, arguing instead that parent-child dynamics are a larger contributor to obesity than an underactive thyroid gland. In 1941, she studied psychiatry at Johns Hopkins University, and from 1943 to 1964, she practiced psychoanalysis at Columbia's College of Physicians and Surgeons. With the publication of *The Importance of Overweight* in 1957, Bruch became a leading expert on both eating too much and eating too little. In 1964, she became a professor of psychiatry at Baylor University School of Medicine in Houston, where she focused her research on the conceptualization, diagnosis, and treatment of anorexia nervosa.

Bruch published the fruits of her decades of research for health professionals in *Eating Disorders: Obesity, Anorexia Nervosa, and the Person Within*. Five years later, she published her research for a general readership in her best-selling book *The Golden Cage: The Enigma of Anorexia Nervosa*. Bruch took the title of the latter from the words of one of her patients, who referred to herself as "a sparrow in a golden cage" since her affluent family had given her so much, yet she felt "deprived of the freedom of doing what she truly wanted." In her posthumously published *Conversations with Anorexics: A Compassionate and Hopeful Journey through the Therapeutic Process*, Bruch focused on the psychoanalytically based treatment of the disorder and presented case studies from her decades of work with those with anorexia and their families.

When Bruch began studying anorexia in the 1950s, there was a wide range of explanations among the experts as to the source of the disorder. Some believed that anorexia isn't a disease but a feature or symptom of an endocrinal disease, such as hypopituitarism. Others believed that the weight loss is a symptom of a psychiatric condition such as schizophrenia, depression, or an obsessional neurosis. "Nervous malnutrition," they called it. In *Holy Anorexia*, Rudolph M. Bell explains that Freud and his followers saw a link between "self-starvation and the sexual drive." By rejecting food, one with anorexia was rejecting an "oral impregnation fantasy involving the father's unincorporated phallus. Eating binges, constipation, and amenorrhea, all typical of anorexia nervosa, respectively symbolize oral impregnation, the child in the abdomen, and the amenorrhea of pregnancy." Paula Saukko, the author of *The Anorexic Self: A Personal, Political Analysis of a Diagnostic Discourse*, succinctly summarizes the positions of what she calls "early doctors" who believed that the disorder is due to "female capriciousness." In other words, anorexia is merely fickle, whimsical, moody female behavior—just what you'd expect from a girl.

Bruch, however, was one of the first to pathologize the condition and establish it as a discrete psychiatric disorder. She contrasted "primary anorexia nervosa" with the "nervous malnutrition" or emaciation that might accompany some other psychiatric diseases. In a 1970 article, Bruch defined primary anorexia as characterized "1) by a relentless pursuit of thinness with body image disturbances of delusional proportions, 2) by a deficit in the accurate perception of bodily sensations, manifest as lack of hunger awareness and denial of fatigue, and 3) by an underlying all-pervasive sense of ineffectiveness." She is credited with being the first to call attention to the fact that those with anorexia have what she called "distorted body images," which has been one of the diagnostic criteria of the disease in the *DSM* since 1980.

Bruch closely observed and analyzed the relationship between the anorectic and her parents, but especially her mother. Here's how Bruch's theory of the mother as perpetrator of her daughter's illness works. Bruch says that the body knows what it needs and communicates that to the brain. Yet there are learned behaviors that interfere with healthy body-mind communication. Bruch interviewed the mothers of those with anorexia and found that most had anticipated their young child's needs rather than allowing the child to feel and express his or her desire for food or attention and then responding to those child-initiated signals. Whether the mother's inappropriate response to those signals is due to neglect, permissiveness, or oversolicitousness, the effect is the same. The children of such mothers are confused about or unaware of their own physical and emotional needs and so are unable to distinguish between theirs and their mother's, which leaves them feeling ineffective or not in control. Instead of relying on internal signals as to when, what, and how much to eat, these children turn to an external source for this information. Because the mothers soothe their children through oral gratification, the children are likely to grow up unable to accurately differentiate hunger and emotional states and so overeat or refuse to eat.

It's not just internal cues about hunger and satiety that the children of such parenting are confused about. Their mothers tend to transgress their children's psychological boundaries by persistently defining for them how they should feel about such personal and emotional issues as who their friends should be and what careers they should prepare for. Such parents often present their children to the world as idealized manifestations of their own aspirations. As a result, children raised with such parenting tend to grow up to be more attentive to how others perceive their needs than to their actual needs, and they teach themselves to want the very things that others are willing to give them. Complicating this is what Bruch calls "excessive closeness and overintense involvement," an abnormal though common pattern of interaction in such families, a pattern that makes it exceptionally hard for the child to separate herself from her mother or parents during her teen years and become a distinct and independent individual.

Whether the mother of a teenager with anorexia is rigid, perfectionistic, domineering, and overinvolved or self-absorbed, detached, unavailable, and uncaring, she values the child more as an extension of herself than as an individual in her own right and so fails to support and encourage her child's natural maturation into adulthood. Some mothers, like Agnes Carpenter, actively discourage the process of separation and individuation in their children by controlling their earnings and using guilt and accusations to keep them from leaving the family home long after the point at which most people their age have been on their own for several years.

Such an upbringing in what Bruch calls "anorexic families" can lead to serious ego deficiencies in the child, resulting in a poor sense of autonomy and control as well as severe cognitive disturbances. Because such children tend not to see themselves as being in control of something as basic as their own bodies, establishing their autonomy as adolescents is a far more formidable task than it is for their counterparts who were raised in healthier families. The anorectic's protest and her means of gaining power and effectiveness come by rigidly and excessively controlling her eating and weight.

There is much about Bruch that I am grateful for. I am grateful that she saw anorexia as a disorder with specific symptoms and signs rather than as something caused by a fear of or a desire for "oral impregnation" in connection with the Electra complex, by an endocrinal disease, or by bad or capricious female behavior. I am grateful that she recognized that what in *The Golden Cage* she calls the "relentless pursuit of thinness" was the "final step" or symptom in a disease that at heart was an effort to gain control of one's life, develop a sense of identity, and be effective in what one undertakes. I am grateful that she believed in fostering the individuation process and building the self-confidence of one with anorexia by having her establish close relationships with people beyond the family as a way to lessen the preoccupation with food, eating, and weight. I'm grateful that in addition to individual counseling, she advocated family counseling as a way of discovering the family's contributions to an eating disorder and helping parents to develop healthy ways of satisfying their own emotional needs rather than relying on their child to fulfill them. But Bruch's theory is lacking. Of course, she couldn't have anticipated the current interest in the genetic and neurobiological causes of anorexia. But she could have acknowledged the extent to which gendered ideals, patriarchal systems, and social context contribute to disordered eating. In *Obsessions: Reflections on Slenderness*, Kim Chernin points out that because Bruch doesn't acknowledge the significance of the fact that eating disorders primarily affect *female* bodies, her theory is missing something crucial. Chernin writes that one may "wonder why Hilde Bruch infers, but does not make a direct connection between anorexia and a fear of being a woman. For it seems evident that anorexics are afraid of becoming, not adults, not teenagers, but women."

Bruch's ideas became mainstream, and other theorists built upon them. For instance, in *Psychosomatic Families: Anorexia Nervosa in Context*, Salvador Minuchin and his coauthors argue that the disorder is not limited to the individual or the mother-daughter relationship. On the contrary, it is a symptom of "an ailing social structure," meaning the family, and the disease is defined "not only by the behavior of one family member, but also by the interrelationship of all family members." In short, the entire family is implicated. Like Bruch, Minuchin analyzed a range of family-therapy sessions to identify the communication patterns typically found in anorexic families. These patterns include excessive tendencies to nurture or protect; rigidity; lack of conflict resolution; failure to acknowledge or address emotional claims; and enmeshment, a relationship in which personal boundaries are weak, permeable, diffused, or undifferentiated. Members of enmeshed relationships are highly reactive to each other's emotions and share inappropriate types of information, with the child in some cases becoming a parent's confidante.

While some research shows that both mothers and fathers of those with anorexia are rated as being less caring than the parents of non-anorectics in a control group, Minuchin's research reveals that the mother of an eating-disordered child may be loving or rejecting or ambivalent. However, in popular culture, there is but one type of mother of a self-starver, and she is portrayed as critical, controlling, and so prone to meddling in her child's life as to be suffocating. In line with this theory, anorexia is seen as a "hunger strike" against parental control or lack of interest or selective interest, especially from the mother. If you love my brother more than me, I'm going to gulp down a handful of laxatives and diuretics. If nobody cares about me, if I can't be in the youth symphony or have a fun, leisurely summer like my friends, I'm going to become small and sick so that you can't help but notice me. So there!

In *The Anorexic Mind*, psychoanalyst Marilyn Lawrence observes that Bruch and other theorists who "emphasize the pervasiveness of the mother-daughter relationship also note that fathers in the families of anorexic patients are somehow absent either physically or emotionally." Even though the father is physically present, the sense of his absence "seems to indicate an absence of his significance, as if there is a feeling that no one, including the father himself, knows or understands what he means or represents." Lawrence found that among the anorectics that she studied, most weren't attached to their fathers, but neither did they express hostility toward them.

Typically, the child with anorexia perceives herself and her mother as the dominant couple or relationship in the household. In "Body, Mother, Mind: Anorexia, Femininity and the Intrusive Object," Lawrence explains that the purpose of this picture of the family from which the father has been excluded and has no function is to protect "the undifferentiated sense of oneness" that the daughter with anorexia feels with the mother. Girls with eating disorders might fantasize about intruding between the parents so that they can reclaim "their special place with mother, untroubled by the presence of father." Not surprisingly, it's when the daughter is separated from her mother that the eating disorder manifests. In my case, the first bout of my malady occurred when my mother went away to the university when I was fifteen. The incident that triggered the second bout occurred during the summer when she was away at a different university, though the severest symptoms occurred after I left her for a job and an independent adult life when I was twenty-four.

The theory of the mother as the chief contributor to the child's anorexia has its critics. Marlene Boskind-White and William C. White Jr., a counselor and a clinical psychologist, respectively, and authors of *Bulimarexia: The Binge/Purge Cycle and Self-Starvation,* say that the established view of the mother as the cause of her daughter's disease is "myopic, destructive, and unjust. In the area of eating disorders, the mothers' overinvolvement in the lives of their daughters is rarely viewed as stemming from the same frustrations and feelings of helplessness and powerlessness that their daughters experience." Randy Schmidt, in *Little Girl Blue,* says that even as a little girl, Agnes Carpenter was a perfectionist. "It bothered her when things didn't go her way. But people were always making decisions for her. She didn't have control and that bothered her." In short, Agnes Carpenter also had a troubled relationship with her mother or parents. Likewise, in *Unbearable Weight: Feminism, Western Culture, and the Body,* Susan Bordo contends, "It's not mothers who are to blame, because they too are children of their culture, deeply anxious over their own appetites and appearance."

There is wisdom in both Bruch's and Minuchin's theories that families that don't communicate honestly and effectively or treat each other with respect can contribute to the genesis and continuance of an eating disorder. Because eating disorders predominantly affect females, it's right to look at the most formative relationship, that of mother and daughter. Because women have, for most of history, been inextricably linked with the growing, harvesting, and preparation of food and the feeding of their families, and literally make food from their bodies in the form of breast milk for their babies, it's also right to consider the relationship between the child and the one who provides her earliest experience of physical nourishment.

Yet there are questions that these theories don't answer to my satisfaction. Why, for instance, do some people translate the anger, frustration, sadness, and guilt of a conflicted parent-child relationship or family system into a self-punishing starvation regimen instead of expressing those feelings in something else that's just as consuming—throwing oneself into tennis or the theater or alcoholism or scrapbooking or religious evangelism or political activism? And why do so many people grow up to be fine, well-adjusted human beings in spite of their flawed families?

In the past few decades, there's been a growing body of evidence that the parents' chief contribution to the child's eating disorder is genetic rather than relational. Some researchers say that the prevalence and incidence rate of anorexia is on the rise, with more new cases appearing, especially among males, younger children, and older women, than in the past, though what actually may be rising is the number of people seeking treatment. Yet, other researchers say that the prevalence and incidence rate of the disease among women has remained steady, which supports a biological and genetic cause for the disease. In a 2007 article, James I. Hudson and his coauthors report that based on face-to-face surveys of household members from 2001 to 2003, a steady 0.9 percent of women develop anorexia at some point in their lifetimes. If the disorder were entirely or partially due to media messages that a woman's worth is determined by the size of her hips and thighs, the percentage would not have remained constant, but would have grown in the past few decades as girls and women received more and more images and messages via cable television, the internet, and social media that, to quote British model Kate Moss, nothing tastes as good as skinny feels. So, too, if dysfunctional families were the primary cause of eating disorders, then the growing number of parents who spend more time interacting with their smartphones than with their children would likely be causing the percentage of the population with eating disorders to skyrocket rather than hold steady.

When I was pregnant, I tried to create the perfect uterine environment for my children so they'd be physically and emotionally healthy and high achievers. I followed a vegetarian diet, did yoga, including a headstand each morning until I was well into my third trimester, meditated, prayed, listened to classical music, cut my caffeine consumption (though probably not enough), and avoided obstetricians who advocated heavy medical intervention. So many things could go wrong, and if something did, it would be my fault. But as my children grew, I realized how much was beyond my control—genetics, the influence of other people, political and educational philosophies, cultural trends—that would have a deeper and more lasting effect on them than what I had or hadn't eaten, drunk, or thought about during my pregnancy.

We yearn for simple black-and-white explanations for our complicated, messy lives. When I encountered the mother-as-perpetrator theory when I was in my twenties, I was glad to have such an easy, simple solution that demanded so little of me and that seemed to explain so much. Even though weighty research points to genetics and biology as the greatest contributors to eating disorders, we're still blaming the mother. But holding to only one cause for a psychosocial disease such as anorexia and other eating disorders is to reduce, minimize, or deny the full reach and complexity of an eating disorder, and it disrespects those who suffer from it. I believe that even in my twenties, I knew on a deep level that the causes of my malady were more multifaceted than simply a single aspect of the parenting I had or hadn't received.

CHAPTER SIX

HARDWIRED

It was in seventh grade that I realized I wasn't like most other kids. One point of difference was that I was so self-conscious that I risked little, for fear of ridicule or rejection. In most classes I didn't raise my hand even when I knew the answer. Another point of difference was that I was strongly introverted. After I spent time with people, I felt frazzled and needed to be alone so that I could recharge. When Dad picked me up from a slumber party, he'd find me sitting on the front step, overnight bag in hand, ready, really, really ready, to go to my bedroom, shut the door, and in the luxurious, velvety solitude, unwind and become myself again. Another way in which I was different from other kids was that I believed in being prepared. When I went out to play as a child, I often carried a little red suitcase or a bindle and stick filled with things that I might need—a comb, a tablet and pencil, Kleenexes, a doll and a change of clothes for her, a View-Master—since I didn't want to be away from home and unprepared even if it was just across the alley to play in the neighbor kids' backyard. I was so young when I started this behavior, I called the little red suitcase my "hoo-case." This behavior has carried over into adulthood. Now I can't leave home without a well-packed purse (toiletries, makeup, first-aid supplies, a spare pair of earrings, a little notebook, and so on) and a bag with plenty to work on—books, drafts of my essays and those of my students, and comfortable shoes and hat in case I want to take a walk. This behavior, then as now, was an antidote, safeguard, or counterbalance to the perils of the unplanned or spontaneous.

As far back as I can remember, I loved rules and structure. Saturday mornings, my mother paid me twenty-five cents for having made my bed every day that week, money that I didn't spend but kept in my Uncle Scrooge bank. I had no complaints about my salary, but the workload concerned me. I wanted Mom to assign me more chores and to ground me if I didn't do them right, but she wasn't cooperative on this count. In fact, she paid me in full whether I made my bed every day or not.

I dreamed of being a servant because I envied the predictable schedule, the firm, clear expectations, and the certainty of repercussions for not toeing the line. I suppose I saw security and order in these constraints. My favorite books were about girls living with rules and duties in orphanages or boarding schools or in poor, hardworking families—Jane Eyre, Annie Sullivan (Helen Keller's teacher), Jo March in *Little Women,* or Cinderella, though once the mistreated stepchild slipped her foot into the glass slipper and went on to the privileged life that accompanied that perfect fit, I lost interest in her. As an adult, I tend to challenge or ignore those rules made by others, and so appear to be a rebellious or uncooperative spouse, employee, church member, or volunteer. But I love my own rules. If I determine that 9:30 is my bedtime, I will forgo free tickets to a play that I want to see if it starts at 8:00. If I determine that because of my sensitive stomach, I can have only a light, early dinner of fruit and yogurt, then a light, early dinner of fruit and yogurt it is. To dine on a spicy meal at a late hour, even if it is in my favorite Thai restaurant, the one with fresh flowers and linen cloths on the tables and the superb panang curry sauce, is to create havoc with my rules, my schedule, my safety, my well-being. If I do go for that late and spicy dinner, I'm edgy and apprehensive because there's always a price to pay for disrupting one's routines and regimens. This inflexibility—or is it constancy?—extends to just about everything in my life, from child rearing to yoga, from religion to romance. But traveling is the worst. When I travel, my rules become even tighter, even nitpickier. By the time I check out three different motel rooms before settling on the one that I find least unsatisfactory, I'm sick of myself and my safeguards from all that could run amuck.

Related to this love of rules is a tendency toward ritualistic behavior. Even though my bedroom was often a little messy when I was a child, I liked certain things to be lined up. The throw rug, for instance, had to be square with the boards in the hardwood floor; no one book could stick out farther on the shelf than the others. If things weren't in line, I felt edgy, anxious, and out of whack. Also, I had to touch some things—a door, the dog, some object that had just called to me—a certain number of times before I was free to leave them. Occasionally, three was the number, but far more often, I was commanded to touch something an even number of times so that "everyone had a friend." On rare occasions, I noticed other people touching or lining up things, so I knew that I wasn't the only person like this. Like me, the other touchers and adjusters engaged in these routines self-consciously, surreptitiously, sheepishly. Through them, I saw how weird my behaviors were.

Also, I sometimes took pleasure in self-denial. If other people didn't treat me right, I punished myself instead of them. You forgot to serve me a piece of that delicious-looking chocolate cake? Then fine, I don't want any. I'll just sit here and not eat, which is going to make you feel really bad. Besides, I kind of deserved to be punished. Certainly this thought pattern was a motivator during the Punishing Summer.

When I taught high school in the 1980s, I found that students with anorexia and bulimia were some of my best students because of their high and rigid need for order, symmetry, and control and their extraordinary work ethic: they would write five pages in their journals for every one page I'd assigned and overprepare not only for tests but even for little pass/fail writing exercises. When Ian was hospitalized in Des Moines for two weeks with a bone infection, Rachel, a student in one of my Advanced Placement Composition classes, visited us. She sat on the floor of the hospital playroom and built tall block towers for Ian to knock down as she told me about the eating-disorders support group she attended. She binged and purged so often that soon, she'd be hospitalized for heart problems at a facility too far away for me to visit. I'd send assignments to her through her mother and receive them back, complete and impeccably done. Such students demanded a lot, and they made complete sense to me. And so do other eating-disordered women and girls. But while I admire their discipline and accomplishments, I find them high-strung and self-conscious. They're not people I could easily spend much time with.

I was and continue to be hard pressed to say anything good about my personality traits. I continue to wonder why I can't just relax and be more like those that I most admire—people who instead of feeling derailed if someone drops by to visit unannounced, enjoy it and feel energized by it; who after exposing themselves through words or actions don't spend the next few days rerunning the episode in their heads until they're bored or exhausted by it; who see the world as a place of abundance rather that scarcity; who trust that things will turn out and if they don't, oh well, it's nothing to stew over.

Four decades after the onset of my malady, I read psychological, neurobiological, and genetic studies about the anorexic brain in hopes of better understanding my own struggles with food restricting and self-image and my anxiety-prone disposition. The conclusions of the research I read fell into two overlapping categories: that certain largely hereditary personality types are strongly associated with eating disorders and that hormones, chemicals, and neural processes send wrong or distorted signals to the anorexic or bulimic brain about hunger and satiety. As I plodded my way through dozens of articles about neurotransmitters and hormones I'd never heard of and about concepts like genetic diathesis, heritability, and familial aggregations of the occurrence of a trait, which I but partially grasped, it struck me that, for so many reasons, those with eating disorders can't trust their brains to tell them the truth about when and when not to eat, when to be anxious or frightened or demanding of themselves and when to let go.

In a 2004 study, Walter H. Kaye, director of the Eating Disorders Research and Treatment Program at the University of California, San Diego; Cynthia Bulik, director of the Center of Excellence for Eating Disorders at the University of North Carolina; and three other researchers studied the comorbidity of anxiety disorders with eating disorders. Comorbidity refers to two or more diseases or other pathological processes that exist simultaneously and usually independently of each other, such as substance abuse and mental illness. The researchers administered standardized tests for anxiety, perfectionism, obsessionality, and eating disorders to 97 individuals with anorexia, 282 with bulimia, and 293 with both disorders, as well as a control group. They found that 66 percent of the members of the three eating-disordered groups had "one or more lifetime anxiety disorders," 41 percent had obsessive-compulsive disorder, and 20 percent had a social phobia. The majority reported that the onset of their anxiety disorder, obsessive-compulsive disorder, or social phobia had occurred during childhood, before the symptoms of their illness manifested. Even those who had recovered from an eating disorder and were symptom-free "still tended to be anxious, perfectionistic and harm avoidant."

In "Is Anorexia Nervosa an Eating Disorder? How Neurobiology Can Help Us Understand the Puzzling Eating Symptoms of Anorexia Nervosa," Kaye and three coauthors conclude that because so many of those with anorexia or bulimia experience an anxiety disorder years before their eating disorder manifests, anxiety is a vulnerability factor or critical pathway for developing these conditions. The perfectionistic and obsessive thinking displayed by many with anorexia and those with "almost anorexia" and other types of disordered eating is often found among their family members who aren't eating disordered, which also points to a genetic cause. Like me, my father was anxious over things that weren't in alignment, weren't exactly right, and he enacted ritualized behaviors to make home and work a little safer, a little more under his control, and to tame the existential chaos. I knew not to interrupt or hurry him when he was checking and rechecking the stove or the door locks or something in the basement. Bulik reminds her readers that behaviors such as restricting and purging that would make most people *more* anxious are experienced as anxiety reducers by those with eating disorders and disordered eating. Self-starvation, then, is a more consequential version of checking the pilot light on the stove multiple times or carrying a little red suitcase when you go out to play.

Perfectionism is another trait strongly associated with eating disorders, expressed both through dissatisfaction with one's body and through rigid thinking. In a 2000 study, Katherine A. Halmi, a professor of psychiatry at Cornell University, and her co-researchers, including Kaye, gave a battery of tests, two for eating disorders, one for obsessive-compulsive disorder, and the Multidimensional Perfectionism Scale, to 322 women with a history of anorexia and a control group of women who had not had anorexia. The subjects with anorexia scored significantly higher on the perfectionism scale than those in the control group. This indicates that perfectionism is a "robust, discriminating characteristic" of the disorder that is likely to be one of a cluster of characteristics that are determined by the interaction of one's genetic makeup and environmental influences.

The results of twin and family studies must be taken with a grain of salt since it's difficult to determine the extent to which heredity alone is responsible for a condition when the subjects have also shared the same home and parents. Even so, the results of twin and family studies suggest a strong genetic component to anorexia. In a review of the various studies done on twins with anorexia, Wade Berrettini, a professor of psychiatry and director of the Center for Neurobiology and Behavior at the University of Pennsylvania Medical School, found that if a fraternal twin has the disorder, the chance of the other twin's developing it is 11 percent. (Genetically, fraternal twins are no more alike than siblings who are not twins.) But when an identical twin has anorexia, the chance of the other twin's also developing the disorder rose to 59 percent. (Identical twins have an identical genetic makeup.) In his review of studies on the occurrence rate among members of an anorectic's immediate family, Berrettini found that they are five to six times more likely to develop an eating disorder than members of the general population. Berrettini concludes that more than half of the risk of developing an eating disorder is due to genetic factors. Similarly, in their study of genetic and environmental influences on disordered eating among adoptees, Kelly L. Klump and her coauthors conclude that twenty-eight out of the thirty twin studies they reviewed suggest "moderate to high heritability (i.e., ~50–85%)" of anorexia and bulimia nervosa and disordered eating.

In the early years of the new millennium, a number of studies appeared concerning the specific chromosomes responsible for anorexia. For instance, Dorothy Grice, a child psychiatrist at the University of Pennsylvania's Center for Neurobiology and Behavior and the first author on a 2002 study of the genetic underpinnings of anorexia nervosa, found suggestive evidence in the thirty-seven families that she and her co-researchers studied that when two or more relatives have the "classic" type of anorexia (restricting but no binging or purging), they found strong evidence for the likelihood of "the presence of an [anorexia]-susceptibility locus on chromosome 1p" and possible linkages on several other chromosomes as well. Bulik, who was part of Grice's research team and who has conducted other studies on the genetics of eating disorders, says that there probably isn't a single gene that "causes" anorexia nervosa. Rather, it's more likely that a number of genes are involved that dispose one to the disorder and so one is more susceptible to environmental triggers—like difficult family dynamics or cultural messages about a female's place and power or about the desirability of being reed thin. When those environmental factors interact developmentally with biologically rooted vulnerabilities like anxiety and perfectionism, a person with a genetic predisposition for developing an eating disorder is at an even higher risk.

Genetics also explain why most eating disorders manifest around the time of puberty or shortly thereafter. Klump and her co-researchers collected saliva from 138 pairs of identical and fraternal adolescent, same-sex twins and assayed the level of estradiol in the samples. Estradiol is the predominant estrogen in females during the reproductive years, and it is the increased production of this hormone during puberty that is largely responsible for genital growth, breast development, and changes in the distribution of body fat in pubescent girls. Also during puberty, estradiol influences a girl's behavior by making permanent changes in her neural structures. Because of these changes, her brain responds to the circulating levels of estradiol in such a way that it influences or activates the expression of eating-disordered behavior. Klump and her co-researchers found that there was little difference in the responses to questions on the Minnesota Eating Behavior Survey about weight preoccupation, body dissatisfaction, binge eating, and compensatory behavior before the start of puberty between identical and fraternal twins with lower levels of estradiol. But among the pairs with higher estradiol levels, the correlation among identical twins in their responses to the survey was more than twice that among fraternal twins—evidence of greater genetic effects. Klump says that these findings provide preliminary support for her hypothesis that "levels of estradiol moderate genetic effects on several types of disordered eating attitudes and behaviors."

Numerous studies show that those with anorexia have abnormally high levels of serotonin, a neurotransmitter that relays messages from one part of the brain to another and is linked to the perception of pain, appetite and digestion, memory, sexual function, temperature regulation, sleep, and some social behaviors. When those with normal serotonin levels endure severe and prolonged periods of food deprivation, they don't get enough of the amino acid tryptophan to manufacture the neurotransmitter. This leaves them feeling anxious and irritable. But Kaye and psychiatrist Theodore E. Weltzin found that when those with anorexia severely restrict their caloric intake, their abnormally high levels of serotonin drop and they report feeling calmer and *less* anxious. In a 2011 study, Ursula F. Bailer and Kaye used brain-imaging technology to study disturbances in serotonin pathways that play a role both in the development of anorexia and bulimia and in the functional changes in the brain associated with those disorders.

Bailer and Kaye conclude that because the alterations were present when the subjects were ill and persisted after recovery, these traits are likely to be independent of the illness. In addition to high levels of serotonin, those with anorexia also have high levels of cholecystokinin and dopamine, two other chemicals that signal satiety in the brain, and low levels of appetite promoters, such as galanin and norepinephrine. This means that the anorectic's brain isn't telling her the truth about what her body needs to be well nourished.

Several studies in recent years have focused on the functioning of the anterior insular cortex as an important cause of eating disorders. In a 2007 article in the *New York Times,* "A Small Part of the Brain, and Its Profound Effects," Sandra Blakeslee describes the insula, a prune-sized slab deep in the brain, as "a sort of receiving zone that reads the physiological state of the entire body and then generates subjective feelings that can bring about actions, like eating, that keep the body in a state of internal balance." The insula is the first area in the cortex to recognize that something one has tasted is sweet, salty, or sour. Along with a related network that includes the amygdala, the ventral anterior cingulate cortex, and the orbitofrontal cortex, the insula tells us whether we find that taste enjoyable or disagreeable. In a study published in 2013, Tyson A. Oberndorfer and several other researchers, including Kaye, gave tastes of sugar to three groups: recovered anorectics, recovered bulimics, and a control group of women who had never had either disorder. They observed the activity in the subjects' insulae through functional magnetic resonance imaging (fMRI) and compared their neural responses. The researchers found that when those in the control group who had never had an eating disorder were given sugar, their right anterior insulae lit up. The more they enjoyed the taste, the more activity there was in that part of the brain. Recovered bulimics had a significantly elevated blood flow in the right anterior insula in response to the taste of sugar, while those who had recovered from anorexia displayed significantly diminished activity in that part of the brain. Oberndorfer and his co-researchers concluded that "restricted eating or overeating may occur because hunger signals aren't being accurately recognized or perceived within the corticolimbic circuits [this includes the insula] involved in appetite regulation."

The increased activity in the insula that the women in the control group displayed in response to a pleasurable taste is a normal response since when we're hungry, our neural networks become more active, which makes food taste more rewarding and drives us to eat. The diminished activity in the insula and other parts of the neural networks in those who have recovered from anorexia indicates that their ability to perceive a taste as pleasing is fundamentally altered. Because they get mixed messages from their brains, those with anorexia may pore over recipes, browse for too long at the grocery store, fantasize or dream about food, and make delicacies for others to eat, and yet not be motivated to eat.

Further evidence that those with anorexia may not be receiving accurate messages about what they are or are not feeling is found in a study led by Irina A. Strigo and her colleagues. They used fMRI to assess the "neural substrates of pain anticipation and processing" in twelve female subjects who had recovered from anorexia and ten female control subjects who had never had the disorder. The researchers attached a thermode to each subject's forearm. A color display showed the intensity of the painful heat stimulus. The researchers observed a mismatch between the pain responses of those who had recovered from anorexia, as measured by the fMRI, and what they said they experienced; this mismatch of responses did not occur in the control group. Strigo and her coauthors say that this discrepancy suggests "altered integration and, possibly, disconnection between reported and actual interoceptive state," or level of sensitivity to stimuli produced within one's own body. The results of this and other studies indicate that those with anorexia have a reduced capacity to accurately perceive signals from the body, including those pertaining to pain, hunger, and satiety. This deficit appears to persist even after one has recovered from the disease.

Any one of these influences—increased tendency toward anxiety, perfectionism, and obsessiveness, higher than normal levels of estradiol at puberty or of serotonin, and various factors that influence the taste of food and the feeling of hunger, fullness, and pain—would be a challenge to manage. But that several or all of these biological influences and more may be co-occurring and interacting with environmental factors explains why full-syndrome anorexia nervosa is such a complex and difficult psychiatric disorder to treat or recover from.

According to the website of the National Eating Disorders Association, "the most effective and long-lasting treatment for an eating disorder is some form of psychotherapy or psychological counseling, coupled with careful attention to medical and nutritional needs." Yet one hopes that treatments based on neurobiological discoveries can enhance or accelerate the healing. For instance, Oberndorfer and his coauthors say that if anorectics have an overly active satiety signal in response to tasty foods, they might be able to eat more if they avoid foods they find especially desirable in favor of those that are "bland, dilute, even slightly aversive." They might consume more calories by eating smaller and more frequent meals to avoid "overstimulation and early satiety." Drugs might be prescribed to modulate the reactivity of the insula and to strengthen the anorectic's responsivity to food or to weaken the bulimic's hyperresponsivity to food. Deep-brain stimulation is being investigated as a way to reformat malfunctioning brain circuitry. And techniques such as biofeedback and mindfulness training can be used to alter the brain's response to food stimuli.

While one can recover from an eating disorder, the research suggests that one doesn't recover from the glitchy hardwiring that contributed to it or the "scars" in the brain that can result from starvation. Those with anorexia, bulimia, or other specified feeding or eating disorders may come into the world too sensitive, too anxious, and with brains that send them incorrect or skewed messages. This knowledge raises conflicting feelings within me. To believe that a malady that has taken me by surprise at three different times in my life is self-inflicted, which is what many people believe about eating disorders and disordered eating, is also to nourish the hope that someday, I'll find the clarity, strength, and self-acceptance to dismantle it, banish it, release it, and be rid of it—not just for the time being, but once and for all. On the other hand, to believe that there's a genetic and biological component to my malady is to be freed from some of the responsibility for it and the puzzlement and guilt I've felt for having "caused" or "created" it. Yet the thought that it's inborn diminishes my hope that I'll ever be free of it. I'm hard pressed to say which position I'd choose—if choosing were an option. But it is not. What I concluded after reading and contemplating the research is that my malady is due to a combination of factors, both those that are within and those that are beyond my control.

During Israel's long journey from Mount Sinai to the Plains of Moab, the southern edge of the Promised Land, God told Moses to send some of his men to "spy out" the land of Canaan, God's gift to the Israelites. Accordingly, Moses sent Joshua, Caleb, and ten other tribal leaders to explore the Promised Land and return with a thorough report of the land, the resources, and those who dwelt there. Upon their arrival at what became known as the Valley of Eshcol (in Hebrew, *eshcol* means "bunch of grapes"), the spies gathered pomegranates and figs, and cut down a branch bearing a single cluster of grapes so large that it took two men to carry it on a pole between them.

When they returned from their forty-day reconnaissance mission, the spies gave their reports to Moses, Aaron, and the Israelites. Joshua and Caleb bore witness to the fertile and bountiful land that awaited them. Just look at the cluster of grapes we brought back! And you should see the great number and enormous size and power of the people who live there and the strength of their cities! The ten other spies, however, emphasized different features in their reports, stirring up dissent among the Israelites with their descriptions of scary giants and little mention of how the land flowed with milk and honey. "We seemed like grasshoppers in our own eyes, and we looked the same to them," the ten men reported.

When the Israelites heard the latter, they were terrified about this place to which God was leading them. All night, they cried out in distress, forgetting all those tender mercies they had received (God's provision of a deliverer, Moses, to lead them out of slavery; God's parting of the Red Sea, which swallowed the pursuing army; God's provision of daily bread and meat during their forty-year sojourn; God's provision of laws that brought order, safety, and a greater degree of certainty into their lives; God's forgiveness after the debacle with the golden calf). God was sending them into a bountiful land where everything—the fruits *and* the foes—grew very, very big. Joshua and Caleb tore their clothes in sorrow at the people's fear and lack of faith and told them that with God's help, the Promised Land was theirs for the taking. The Israelites were on the verge of stoning Joshua and Caleb when God appeared over the Tent of the Tabernacle. God was so angry with his complaining, ungrateful people that he was ready to strike them with a plague, but once again, Moses changed God's mind.

What I appreciate about this story is how it shows that when presented with the same data, people reach such different conclusions. Some focused on the giant grapes, others on the giant people. Some, after witnessing God's many blessings upon them during their desert wanderings, chose to trust God, while others did not. Their different responses were due both to their life experiences and to their brain chemistry or hardwiring. This story calls me to push against my hardwired pessimism so that I can see *everything* that is before me, whether I judge it as good and desirable or not, and to be open to possibilities. If one is looking only for what is threatening or not up to snuff, she'll find it.

Kate, a wise therapist I worked with from 2006 until 2011, listened patiently to me as I complained yet again about my personality type. Lining things up. Following rules. Tending to the details. Analyzing and reanalyzing my own behavior. On the sidelines, observing and taking notes. After all these years, after all this therapy, I'm still trying to take care of myself in this curious way. "Yes, all of those things are true," Kate said. "And so is this. You probably wouldn't have written all those books and essays or be such a good teacher or sacrificed so much for your children, if you had been wired differently." I was stunned, not by this realization but by the fact that it had never before occurred to me: my personality traits have caused me anguish, but they've also borne good fruit, giant clusters of giant grapes.

CHAPTER SEVEN

CRAVINGS

When I remember the seven-year period between 1984, when I was pregnant with Ian, and January of 1991, when Meredith was born, I see myself as almost well, almost healthy, almost normal in terms of how and what I ate. My symptoms weren't gone, but they'd lessened in frequency and severity. Sometimes I binged or restricted or exercised for too long, but my weight was normal and stable. Sometimes I felt frozen and fogged in after I ate, but I didn't hide food and only occasionally threw it away out of fear that someone had tainted it. As my fear of tainted food lessened, I enjoyed intervals of relative stability punctuated by occasional, stress-triggered flare-ups of symptoms. While at the time, I may not have been able to explain why my food fears and restrictions began loosening their hold on me, now I suspect that the demands of motherhood gave me the boundaries and restrictions that I craved and shifted most of my attention from myself onto my children. And, too, I became more successful at identifying and responding to my deep hungers. Now I think of these seven years as a transitional period, a time when I was moving from sickness to wellness, a time of partial remission from my malady. I didn't know then whether my release from the worst symptoms of my malady was temporary or permanent. I was just grateful they had subsided.

Not that I was ever symptom-free. My disordered-eating behaviors and thoughts were always there to some degree, but these kinks and quirks affected my life in ways that were manageable and that I could hide or camouflage. Never during this seven-year period did I hear the click and feel the shift, followed by the easy restricting and that exhilarating rush of power and purpose it put into play. But I was worried—not so much that someone would taint my food or drink but that once again I would become *afraid* that someone would do this to me. Fear is what I feared. To me, wellness meant no longer being afraid.

What most marks this transitional time are my cravings, those longings, yearnings, hankerings, and hungers that overwhelmed other thoughts, ordered my days, filled my dreams, determined my reading lists, and placed me not in the here and now but in the distant future, where, surely, I'd find fulfillment. My most urgent desires were for ordinary, physical food, of course, but also for God, social justice, and the ability to tell the world about all of this through poems and essays. I sometimes felt that my ambitions were too narrow, my home too cramped, my skin too taut, the bones of my skull too tight. My soul, pent up in a small, circumscribed space, wanted to expand like those tight little origami flowers that unfurl when you drop them in water. I took it as a sign of healing that what I was yearning to fill myself with was more than just ordinary food and that as I attended to my other hungers, the symptoms of my malady subsided.

Because of these restless cravings, I changed addresses and employers several times during this seven-year period. First I moved from Omaha to Burlington so I could live with my parents in the months leading up to and following Ian's birth. When Ian was seven days old, I entered the graduate program in Composition and Rhetoric in the English Department at Western Illinois University in Macomb, Illinois, one hour east of Burlington. To cover my tuition and earn a stipend, I tutored in the Writing Lab and taught freshman composition. I was surprised by how different and so much more satisfying it was to teach adults than fifteen-year-olds. When I taught high school, I not only taught the subject matter and graded my students' work but also monitored the cafeteria or hallway during my "free" period, filled out piles of forms, managed discipline problems, met with parents and counselors, tried to motivate reluctant or disinterested learners, and provided enrichment for willing and interested students. I found that college teaching was almost entirely focused on the subject matter and that I could do much of my work at home. During the first semester of my program, Ian and I lived with my parents and I commuted. But during the other three semesters, we lived in Macomb, where I learned to balance the demands of caring for a baby, studying, writing a thesis, and teaching.

After I received my master's degree, I applied for teaching positions at community colleges and a few universities. What I wanted to do was write poems and essays and teach adults to do the same. But no one from any of the search committees called me for an interview. As a backup plan, I'd applied at a few high schools, even though I was sure that I didn't want be locked into such a demanding schedule and workload. Because my son and I needed a steady paycheck, health insurance, and our own place, it was with resignation that I accepted a good position at a high school in West Des Moines, Iowa. Just days before Ian's second birthday, we moved into a four-room duplex in south Des Moines. When I'd lived in Iowa City, Omaha, and Macomb, I'd always had an escape: I could cut my losses, pack up, and go home whenever I wanted. But now there was no going back. Real, adult life had irrevocably begun. Between single parenting Ian and working my demanding job (I had three new class preparations each day: sophomore English, Individualized Reading, and Advanced Placement Composition, the latter of which was exceptionally demanding in terms of the grading and class preparations, although it was also stimulating and gratifying), I was exhausted and frazzled. I had little time for writing, much less socializing or just sitting on a chair beneath the big silver maple in my backyard and contemplating.

During my second winter in Des Moines, I had frequent and vivid dreams, some cool and buoyant, some glowing and feverish, about moving to New Mexico or California, so I applied to graduate programs in these places. As a backup plan, I also applied to a few midwestern universities. The school that wanted me enough to provide a good teaching assistantship was the University of Nebraska–Lincoln (UNL), located not near mountains or an ocean but on what had been salt flats and tallgrass prairie, a place that never once appeared as the setting of or the object of desire in my dreams. I wouldn't be leaving the white-bread Midwest after all, but at least I was going a little farther west than Des Moines. Finishing my PhD wasn't my priority. I was going to graduate school because I craved freedom from a demanding, sixty-hour-a-week job so that I could devote more of myself to writing spare, luminous poems and to mothering Ian, who seemed hungry for more time with me. Lincoln was but an interlude, a period of repose, a for-the-time-being place. I imagined that what was beyond graduate school involved teaching in a college in some western or southwestern place.

When, at age fifteen, I gained so much weight so fast in the upper outer parts of my thighs, the dermis, or middle layer of skin, which is made up of strong, stretchy interconnected fibers, became overstretched and thin. This caused tiny tears or breaks, which allowed the blood vessels to show through. When these stretch marks first appeared, they were purple or red and looked like violent, painful tears. But as the blood vessels eventually contracted, the fat beneath the skin showed through, so the stripes or striae turned silvery white. Now when I remember the seven-year period of growing wellness, I see it as a time when I desired so much, and grew and stretched so rapidly, that it left dark red-purple stretch marks on my intellect, heart, spirit, and soul.

My weight was normal, but my appetite was not. I craved bread, both homemade and factory made. I craved ice cream, pudding, cakes, cookies, pies, doughnuts, pancakes. I craved potatoes: mashed, baked, scalloped, pan fried; in salad, soup, or stew; fried with eggs or just boiled and salted. I was ravenous. But I was afraid that if I ate "normally," my appetite would overpower me and I'd be fat again. Consequently, I became an expert, of sorts, at responding to both of my desires—to eat and to not gain weight.

When I was at work or school, I ate raw carrots or apples for lunch, or, just as often, I ate nothing between breakfast and supper. I no longer ate homemade bread for breakfast since I had no restraint when there was a loaf in the house. All or nothing. Instead, each day I ate more servings of a laxative cereal than I want to admit to so that what I did eat left my body before I had had time to absorb all the calories. I rarely baked sweets or brought tempting items like ice cream into the house. If Ian wanted a treat, I'd take him to the grocery store or bakery for a cookie or doughnut or ice cream bar. If I bought bread for Ian's meals, I kept it in the scary basement of my duplex or the trunk of my car, which made it a little harder for me to get at than if it was on the counter or in the freezer. Even so, I sometimes binged. What kind of example was I setting for my son, I wondered.

Each day, I walked and biked many miles, mostly with Ian either in the stroller or, later, in the child's seat on my bike. When he was in preschool, I'd take him to school and then leave my car parked there so I could walk to and from the university, which took almost an hour each way. If I couldn't exercise on the weekend because the weather was too cold, snowy, or rainy for Ian to be out, I was edgy and keyed up, my muscles starchy and itchy, until I discovered that a combination of jogging and doing jumping jacks on a small trampoline, followed by aerobic yoga—one sun salutation after another—was almost as good as taking a long bike ride. Occasionally I feared that I'd been poisoned and would not eat, or I threw food out, or I felt gray, dizzy, and brain-fogged after I ate.

I nursed Ian until well after his third birthday, though toward the end of this time, it was more of a token act before he went to bed in the evening than anything substantive. Of course, breast-feeding has numerous health benefits for the mother and child and strengthens the emotional bond between them, but I can't claim that my motives were purely selfless. Years later I would read about women who express more milk than their baby needs so they can lose weight or who continue expressing their breast milk after they've weaned their babies or toddlers as a way of burning an additional five hundred or so calories per day. "Extreme breast pumping," it's called. Though I never went to such extremes, I did suspect that prolonged breast-feeding was yet another way of preventing a gain in weight. Though these methods of keeping my weight down weren't dangerous or abnormal, they seemed to me to be just a little odd or off center.

When Ian was two or three, we went to a health fair, where medical students tested his vision and hearing and gave him a dental hygiene coloring book and a toothbrush. The students took my vitals and analyzed a questionnaire I completed about what I ate in an average day. Occasionally, I binged on bread. But since bingeless days were far more typical, I recorded what I ate on those days. The student who discussed my results with me recommended that I increase my food intake by several hundred calories per day. I was pleased to hear that I wasn't eating enough. He was especially concerned that I hadn't menstruated since I became pregnant with Ian. I supposed that that was due as much to lactation and excessive exercise as to not eating enough food. Someday I would achieve balance, I thought, but in the meantime, I had no intention of eating differently.

During this time of almost normal eating, I worked with four different therapists, a different one in each of the cities and towns in which I lived. Sometimes we talked about my disordered eating. But more often, we talked about my hardwiring, my anxieties, my family, and Gerald, who ignored Ian most of the time but occasionally showed up with some cockamamie plan for the two of us to get back together that involved his traveling as much as he wanted but having a key to my apartment. Though therapy didn't fix anything, by analyzing my problems and personality type with my therapists, I did come to know myself better, so I kept going back.

Sometimes I went to meetings of Overeaters Anonymous (OA), an elegantly simple twelve-step program that asked me to abstain from "compulsive eating," a catchall category that included all the varieties of disordered eating, not through willpower or intellectual analysis but by surrendering control of my "addiction" to God or my higher power. OA demanded wholehearted trust and moment-by-moment awareness and surrender, but little analysis. Based on the stories I heard at the meetings from people who had gained the power through surrender to lessen or stop their restricting, binging, or binging and purging, or simply eating more than they should, I knew that this approach had the potential to transform everything in my life. But I wasn't yet ready or willing to stop living in the future and "be here now," as Ram Dass advised, or to give up my kinks and quirks.

I craved more of God. During this time of remission, I was religiously eclectic, borrowing from Christianity, Hinduism, and any other system that brought me closer to God. I didn't yet consider myself to be a Christian (I fell short in so many ways), but I became a regular churchgoer, something that I hadn't intended to do, something that surprised me.

I started going to church after Ian was born for primarily secular reasons. Because I had fond memories from my childhood of the social aspects of Sunday school, Bible school, ice cream socials, potlucks, and trick or treating for UNICEF with the youth group, church involvement seemed like a good way to provide my son with some of the people connections that were lacking in a single-parent, one-child home. And, too, I was grateful for a couple of hours on a Sunday morning when Ian, an extremely active and inquisitive child, could play and learn with the other kids in the nursery and Sunday school, and I could sit with adults in the church service and the discussion group that followed. Many weekends, this was the only time that he and I were apart. Also, I wanted my son to have a value system that he could accept or reject or revise as he saw fit. When I taught high school, I saw students who'd not been given a moral-ethical belief system. Theirs was an ungroundedness that made normal teenage rebellion more difficult. Rebels with nothing meaningful to rebel against. Mainstream, white-bread Christianity gave a teenager plenty to push against. My son would have that.

When I was in graduate school at Western Illinois University, Ian and I often spent our weekends in Burlington. We'd go with my father and occasionally Great-Aunt Pertsie to their small Methodist church, where the pastor gave amusing, mildly inspiring sermons and we sang the old familiar hymns that I'd grown up with, as well as some new ones. Before and after the services, people shook our hands, asked questions about Ian, and kidded him a bit. On those weekends when we stayed in Macomb, Ian and I went to an unaffiliated Baptist church that I was led to through the friend of a fellow graduate student. I was impressed that these off-brand Baptists not only warmly received the adults with intellectual disabilities who were unwelcome at other churches in town but also picked them up at their group home on Sunday mornings; instead of segregating them in their own class, they included them in the same Sunday school class as all the other adults; and they drove them home after fellowship. The Jesus that I met at the Baptist church was a best friend, a constant companion, a source of love, support, and joy, and the humble servant of those Jesus called "the least of these" (Matthew 25:40).

During the two years that I taught in West Des Moines, I was a member of the Methodist church in our south Des Moines working-class neighborhood. The social aspects of the church were pretty white bread, with most folks focused on the demands of work, bills, and family. Church provided tradition and life-passage rituals for them. But Pastor Strong was a robust, filling brown bread, made from unmilled grains, raw honey, nuts, and seeds. I took notes during his passionate, substantive sermons on the parables of Jesus and the Sermon on the Mount that called for social justice and action. During the week, I returned to the scriptural passages and studied them through this new lens. When we prayed, "Thy kingdom come, thy will be done, on earth as it is in heaven," it was an urgent prayer with an expectation of fulfillment here and now rather than in ages to come. When I encountered the concept of liberation theology, focused as it was not on salvation in the afterlife but on this time and place through repair of unjust social structures and the misery they created, I realized that I'd been given a name for Pastor Strong's approach to the Gospel. In *A Theology of Liberation* (1971), the Peruvian priest Gustavo Gutierrez Merino, widely regarded as the founder of liberation theology, declared, "I desire that the hunger for God may remain, that the hunger for bread may be satisfied." That was my prayer. The Jesus that I encountered at the Methodist church in south Des Moines was the Great Liberator of the oppressed and marginalized, freeing "the least of these" from the political and social injustices that held them in bondage.

While I lived in Des Moines, I dated Andy, who believed that divine healings occurred during the noisy, joyous charismatic masses that he participated in, held on Wednesday evenings in a small chapel far from the main sanctuary of an old Catholic church in downtown Des Moines. I was open to the possibility of sudden and complete healing, yet I didn't step up to the railing, didn't allow the healer to lay hands on me, didn't fall back into an assistant's arms, to be laid on the floor, slain in the spirit, whole and healed. Was I afraid of the public attention, or did I not *want* a sudden and complete healing? Each weekday morning before Andy went to work, he helped serve free breakfasts in the basement of an inner-city church to kids on their way to school, a beautiful enactment of the Gospel message. Could I also live the Gospel message in such a profound way?

I craved social justice. Between my job and caring for Ian, I found it difficult to voice my support for nuclear disarmament, economic justice, and human rights through protests, vigils, and other public forms of political action. But I could and did write letters both to my elected officials and to the leaders of other countries, such as P. W. Botha, the South African prime minister and president who maintained the system of apartheid; José Napoleón Duarte, the El Salvadoran president whose citizens were terrorized and massacred by the military's death squads; and the leaders of those countries that, according to Amnesty International, held prisoners of conscience. I didn't have the satisfaction of interacting with the hungry children I'd just served food to, as Andy did, but when I dropped a letter in the mailbox, I felt some peace for having acted on my beliefs.

I'd always been interested in politics and world affairs, and even in middle school, I read the newspaper. In high school, I wrote research papers not on the physical evidence for reincarnation or controversies surrounding the death of Jim Morrison or which breed of dog makes the best pet but on the Alaska pipeline, which I opposed, and the population explosion, which I believed should be controlled. Though I'd voted in all the major elections, when I lived in Des Moines, I paid close attention to the promises being made by those candidates seeking to be my party's nominee for the US presidency. I found one, Jesse Jackson, who, more than any of the others, seemed to have a deep understanding of poverty and who promised to work to end economic violence, to confront corporate power with populist power, and to advocate for "the least of these." Pastor Strong opened our church to Rev. Jackson, making it the first place he spoke during the months leading up to the 1988 caucuses. With Ian in tow, I volunteered at Jackson's campaign headquarters, and I literally took a stand for my candidate at the Iowa caucuses.

When I moved to Lincoln for graduate school, I became a member of one of the historic peace churches, which taught that because peace is the will of God, all war is sin. As conscientious objectors, members of that denomination were granted exemption from military duty. I was proud to raise my children in such a church and among such people. I dated a member of the Socialist Workers Party, a man who was so passionate about the necessity of an empowered working class that rather than seeking a job that required his bachelor's degree in biology, he worked at a local factory so that he could be active in a labor union. I embraced many of the beliefs of the Socialist Workers Party about economic oppression, yet found the party's expression of their beliefs to be crude and strident, even inflammatory. I turned instead to Nebraskans for Peace, the oldest statewide organization in the country dedicated to peace and justice. I participated in rallies at the state capitol or the governor's mansion in support of numerous causes, including nuclear disarmament, abolition of the death penalty, and the need to reserve water in the Platte River and the Ogallala Aquifer for wildlife and recreation as well as for irrigated agriculture. Through my involvement with these causes, I met wonderful people who had found positive, meaningful ways to set themselves apart from the dominant, mainstream white-bread culture. I brought Ian and Meredith along with me, so from an early age, they saw people speaking truth to power. I prayed for peace and justice and that God's kingdom would soon be in our midst. Sometimes I thought I heard or felt a weakening in the foundation of the old order. I imagined the crumbling and collapse that would follow and allow a new, more peaceful and equitable order to be born.

During this time of partial remission, I yearned mightily to become a writer. What I craved was the ability to bring forth something true and beautiful about my experiences and perceptions, and I hankered after readers who would be moved by my words and ideas. When Ian was a baby and a toddler, the only writing time I had was during my brief lunch period at the high school or during my office hours at the university. Then, I wrote short poems, one of which I saw published in a regional journal. But sometimes my poems grew long and wide until they became brief nonfictional prose accounts and reflections. "Little things," I called them.

At UNL, I entered the doctoral program with the intention of crafting a collection of poetry to fulfill the requirements of the "creative dissertation." During my first year in the program, I took poetry-writing seminars, where my poems became more nimble, more daring, more refined. At the same time, I was still writing "little things," three- to four-page essays about the Farmer's Market, my cast iron kettle, watching a movie about ninja turtles with Ian, attending a bluegrass festival with my parents and Ian, buying a rocking chair at an estate auction, and the human and natural wonders that I saw in and around the two creeks I walked over each weekday on my journey between Ian's preschool and the university. Just common, daily events. I delighted at seeing my name and words in print in *Iowa Woman, Friendly Woman* (a Quaker periodical), the *Des Moines Register,* the Burlington *Hawk Eye,* and other publications. One of my first published pieces was an essay entitled "Why I Bake Bread," about the Saturday morning bread-baking ritual that I'd started when I lived with Stevie in Omaha and sometimes still participated in:

> I appreciate process—growing a garden, composing an essay, teaching a new skill or concept to my two-year-old . . . or baking a loaf of bread. Every time, I recognize a sameness and uniqueness that somehow assures me of the certainty and mystery in my own life. For instance, I have come to expect the dry yeast granules to fizz and foam when I resurrect them with warm water. And after having nourished them with flour and honey and moisture and warmth, I expect to return to my kitchen and find the dish towels bulging with two yeasty risings. I appreciate all of this when it works and even more when it doesn't work. Then I am reminded of the delicate interplay between all those variables in my own life that I can and cannot control.

Several of my earliest published essays were about eating food, preparing food, growing food, and understanding food as substance and symbol. Over twenty-five years later, I still haven't exhausted the subject.

What I learned rather by accident is that these "little things" could be my "real" writing. One day, I stopped in the English Department lounge at UNL to peruse the composition textbooks that a publishing-house representative had put on display. He asked me if I wanted a free copy of *The Best American Essays 1988,* edited by Annie Dillard and Robert Atwan. Sure, I said. I'll always take a free book. Little did I know that this book would change my life by introducing me to the rich world of the personal essay.

When Ian and I went to Burlington for our winter break, I took the anthology with me. Because my parents and Ian were hungry for time together, I had what for me was an extravagant amount of time to read and write. I immersed myself in the selections in *The Best American Essays.* In the introduction to the anthology, Dillard said that she chose essays for this volume that were "a kind of subgenre, the narrative essay" because she was "especially interested in narrative essays that mix plain facts and symbolic facts, or that transform plain facts into symbolic facts." She also noted that many of these writers "narrate in fragments linked by idea." Until then, I had thought that only poets could work with symbolic facts and associative leaps. As I pondered Dillard's introduction and read the essays that followed, Bernard Cooper's "Beacon's Burning Down," Susan Mitchell's "Dreaming in Public: A Provincetown Memoir," Anne Carson's "Kinds of Water," and Albert Goldbarth's "After Yitzl," I realized that essays came from the same imaginative place as poems and short stories and novels and could rely on the same approaches and stylistic techniques. "An essay can do everything a poem can, everything a short story can, everything but fake it," Dillard declared.

During the last two weeks of December 1989 and the first week of January 1990, I read the essays in Dillard's anthology, walked country roads, and wrote on a rented manual typewriter about the pheasants I'd been watching and the reflections and ruminations they inspired. I revised extensively, trying some of the techniques and methods of development that I saw in the essays in Dillard's anthology. What I produced wasn't a mere three or four pages—a little thing—but eleven: a fully developed, grown-up literary essay. "Pheasant Country" was accepted at two of the three literary quarterlies to which I submitted it (I chose to publish it in the University of Oregon's *Northwest Review*), and it received a notable essay nomination for *The Best American Essays of 1991,* edited by Joyce Carol Oates and Robert Atwan. This provided external validation for what I already knew: I wanted to read and write artful, imaginative personal essays; I wanted to teach others to do the same. All I needed was time to practice my art and craft.

I hungered for so much during this time of growth spurts and stretch marks. I wasn't full, but I was far closer than I'd ever been to knowing what I was hungry for and where and how to find it.

During this transitional time of increasing wellness, I read and thought about eating disorders. Given the changes in, or rather the expansions of, my hungers, I started questioning the theory that dysfunctional parents or family are largely to blame for one's unhealthy relationships with food, size, body image, and self. Nor was I willing to place all the blame on the beauty, diet, fashion, and entertainment industries, as many do. But certainly those industries bear partial responsibility since they are both responding to and perpetuating our cultural obsession with thinness, which at its core, says Naomi Wolf, is "an obsession about female obedience."

What profoundly influenced my thinking about the causes and meaning of my malady were the ideas of two writers that I discovered within a few years of each other, Caroline Walker Bynum and Maggie Helwig, each of whom examined the historic reasons for fasting—spiritual perfection and sociopolitical protest, subjects that I was already inclined to think and read about and practice. In a seminar on medieval women mystics at UNL, I chose to do my class presentation on Bynum's *Holy Feast, Holy Fast: The Religious Significance of Food to Medieval Women.* In her study of the cultural and symbolic dimensions of the extreme fasting undertaken by women in religious orders in Western Europe between 1200 and 1500, Bynum discovered that medieval attitudes about food were "far more diverse than those implied by the modern concepts of anorexia nervosa and hysteria." For medieval religious women, abstaining from or restricting food was "a way of controlling as well as renouncing both self and environment." And it was more. Bynum observes that "in renouncing ordinary food and directing their being toward the food that is Christ, women moved to God not merely by abandoning their flawed physicality but also by becoming the suffering and feeding humanity of the body on the cross, the food at the altar." Thus, a woman's refusal to eat was the central vehicle, the metaphor and the method, in her search for identity, relationship, authority, and direct, unmediated connection with God.

After reading Bynum, I delved into the life of Catherine of Siena (1347–1380), who reputedly feasted on nothing but the Eucharist meal and God's love for ten years. Catherine's first fast was in response to her parents' insistence that she not take religious orders as she desired but that she marry the brutal husband of her late sister, Bonaventura. After Catherine lost half of her body weight, her parents dropped their demands, and at age fifteen, she became a lay Dominican sister. According to another story, it was a miraculous and severely disfiguring case of smallpox that struck Catherine when she was seventeen that enabled her to convince her mother that she should join a group of Dominican laywomen. Either way, Catherine tended to the sick, including those struck with the bubonic plague, and drew a wide following to her teachings, austerities, and contemplative practices, one of which involved teaching her followers how to build an "internal cell" within the self where they could go to meditate.

While the Catholic Church sanctioned the ancient discipline of fasting as a form of asceticism, and while in the Sermon on the Mount, Jesus spoke about the proper attitude when practicing this expected discipline (one's suffering should be obvious to God alone, not *if* but *when* one fasts), Catherine's superiors felt that she had taken the discipline to extremes and ordered her to eat. She complied, but each time she put food into her mouth, she promptly heaved it out. By abstaining from food, except for the Communion bread, she identified with Christ's suffering and wed herself to him. Thus, her suffering was made sublime. Some found Catherine's asceticism worthy of respect and veneration. Others were threatened by it.

Catherine's austerities not only deepened her dependence on God but also granted her access to earthly powers that few other women of her time could claim. For instance, in 1376, Catherine traveled to Avignon, France, where seven successive popes had resided, to confer with Pope Gregory XI about returning the papacy to Rome and reuniting Italy and the church; about sponsoring another crusade against "base unbelievers" so that Christians could "possess what is rightfully ours" (the Holy Land); about reforming the clergy, who Catherine said should be "a mirror of voluntary poverty, meek as lambs, distributing the possessions of [the] Holy Church to the poor" instead of living in "luxury and state and pomp and worldly vanity." Catherine saw the papacy returned to Rome, but her other requests went unmet. She also predicted the Great Schism, a time of rival claims to the papacy, and consulted with Pope Urban VI in Rome about ending it.

Medievalist Elizabeth Alvilda Petroff describes Catherine as "a woman of great strength and personal magnetism, a leader who attracted many followers." But surely some of her worldly power was due to the fact that she ate nothing but the Communion wafer. "Father, I am hungry; for the love of God give this soul her food, her Lord in the Eucharist," she told her confessor. In 1380, when Catherine was thirty-three, she suffered a stroke; eight days later, she died. Surely malnourishment contributed to her death. Catherine was canonized eighty-one years later, and in 1970, the Catholic Church declared her a Doctor of the Church, the same honor that it gave to Augustine, Thomas of Aquinas, and St. John of the Cross. Because she was such a prolific writer (385 of her letters survive), her influence continues.

The second writer who shaped my thinking about the meaning of my malady was the Canadian poet, novelist, essayist, and human rights activist Maggie Helwig. Like therapist Salvador Minuchin, Helwig blames an "ailing social structure" for eating disorders. But unlike Minuchin, who identifies that structure as the "psychosomatic family," Helwig is after bigger game. In her 1989 essay "Hunger," which I first encountered in a copy of *Best Canadian Essays 1990* that my fiancé, Marc, bought me when he was attending a conference in Canada, Helwig argues that the popular theories about domineering mothers and our society's "thin is beautiful" fetish trivialize eating disorders. Helwig, who suffered from anorexia for eight years and almost died from it, says that it is no accident that the widespread appearance of eating disorders in the 1960s and the epidemic of the 1970s coincided with the unprecedented growth of the consumer society, which places the highest value on buying and owning things. Helwig observes that by the end of the 1960s, our material consumption had become "very nearly uncontrollable." What resulted is "what is possibly the most emotionally depleted society in history, where the only 'satisfactions' seem to be the imaginary ones, the material buy-offs." Anorexia, then, is the evil of consumerism played out in women's bodies. To that, I would add, so, too, bulimia (interrupting the act of consumption by rejecting and hurling out the food one has taken in) and binge eating disorder (consuming as much as one can, as fast as one can). "It is these women," writes Helwig, "who live through every implication of our consumption and our hunger and our guilt and ambiguity and our awful need for something real to fill us. . . . We have too much; and it is poison." By not eating, the anorectic causes a cessation in ovulation and menstruation, rendering herself literally unproductive. By not eating, the anorectic refuses to be consumed by the act of consumption. Such self-denial in a culture of plenty is an audacious, radically countercultural act and statement. We watch with terror and fascination and admiration.

Everywhere I look, it seems, I see people with the diseases, discomforts, and dislocations that result from consuming more food than the body needs and more of this small planet's resources than is just. The widely held belief in our late capitalist consumer culture that every human appetite, whether for food, sex, petroleum, electronics, entertainment, diversion, consolation, revenge, or convenience, must be satisfied at once can't fill a hungry heart or lessen the pain one feels from isolation, rejection, or a lack of meaning or purpose. Ironically, or perhaps fittingly, what we're really hungry for can't be bought. Most people eat or overeat in response to this hunger. But some starve in the midst of material plenty. Instead of making herself bigger through consumption, the girl or woman with anorexia makes herself smaller since she would rather be skeletally thin than ingest something that isn't real or substantial or safe. Beware of the leavening of the Pharisees, the Herods, the capitalists, the materialists. The bread raised by their yeast not only can't nourish you but will corrupt you and make you very sick.

Just a few weeks before the beginning of the Punishing Summer in 1972, forty members of the provisional Irish Republican Army (IRA), imprisoned for their efforts to end British rule in Northern Ireland, launched a hunger strike in Her Majesty's Prison (HMP) Crumlin Road. By that point, I was a regular reader of the newspaper and so I followed the plight of the strikers with curiosity and uneasiness. What Billy McKee and the others were protesting was their treatment as criminals rather than as prisoners of war. McKee's hunger strike ended on day thirty-six, when the British government relented and conferred prisoner of war status on imprisoned members of the IRA. But eventually, the British government would renege and attempt to weaken the IRA's influence by once again criminalizing its imprisoned members. In 1982, ten hunger strikers in HMP Maze fasted unto death, at which point the strike ended mostly because the family members of the remaining strikers said that they would intervene should their loved ones slip into a coma. Bobby Sands, who was the face of the protest for me, was the first striker to die. He lost sixty pounds in nine weeks. At the time of his death at age twenty-seven, he weighed ninety-five pounds and his skin was pocked with bedsores. How could one care so much about an issue that one would voluntarily turn one's body into a symbol, a metaphor, a living sacrifice? Could that happen to me?

Simone Weil, whom I discovered in my early twenties, was another hunger striker whose story captivated and haunted me. Weil was born into a Jewish family in 1909 but later became an ardent though not baptized Catholic, a brilliant though controversial Christian theologian, a political activist, and a zealous ascetic. For Weil, spirituality and political activism were inseparable. In *Waiting for God,* a collection of Weil's letters and essays that were compiled after her death by two friends, a theologian and a priest, the latter her confessor of sorts, Weil says, "At the center of the human heart is the longing for an absolute good, a longing which is always there and is never appeased by any object in this world." She wasn't willing to consume or be consumed by something that couldn't nourish her. Nor was she willing that anyone should go hungry. She left her academic job for the factory assembly line so she could understand why the French industrial working class was so submissive; to study farm labor, she harvested grapes and potatoes; and she briefly served in a militia unit in the Spanish Civil War. During World War II, Weil restricted so she could give her food coupons or rations to those who had less. What remained, she sent to local internment camps where the Vichy regime, the right-wing, authoritarian government that came to power after France fell to the Nazis, housed political prisoners. When Weil and her family sought safety in New York City in 1942, she decided that she would not eat any more than her rationed compatriots in Marseilles were able to eat, but her biographers agree that she probably ate far less.

In her theological writings, Weil sought to resolve the apparent polarities that she saw between freedom and necessity, God and world, grace and gravity, the last being the title of one of her books. One point that I found particularly provocative was the distinction she made between the polarities of "looking" and "eating." For Weil, eating was a metaphor for the self-centered fulfillment of desire. In *Waiting for God,* she explains that through the act of eating the object of our desire, we cannot see what we desire; rather, we see only ourselves and feed only our perception of ourselves. We desire the good and the beautiful. Yet we can only know these qualities from a distance. By trying to possess, consume, or eat them, our desires remain unfulfilled, and in the process, we destroy what we eat. The only way we can achieve what we truly desire at the core of our being is by looking, paying attention, and waiting for God to take the initiative and come to us in grace.

Attending or looking is challenging because it requires us to maintain what Weil calls "a tension of opposing tendencies." According to Christopher J. Frost and Rebecca Bell-Metereau in *Simone Weil: On Politics, Religion, and Society,* Weil believed that by choosing not to prematurely close the gap between looking and consuming, one could intentionally remain "in this state of perceptual openness." Frost and Bell-Metereau explain, "A key to the mystery of her life and her death, is her perception of life as equivalent to being hungry yet refusing to eat, that is, as a polarity of looking (attending, without closure) versus eating (consuming, with immediate closure)."

Weil also uses the eating metaphor to explore the ways in which humans love each other. "Instead of loving a human being for his hunger, we love him as food for ourselves. We love like cannibals. To love purely is to love the hunger in a human being. Then, since all men are always hungry, one always loves all men." Because we tend to see others only in terms of our own interests, we hurry to assimilate them as part of our own egos. As such, we are not really loving them but loving ourselves instead. The act of "eating," says Weil, is the origin of human sin. "It may be that vice, depravity and crime are nearly always, in their essence, attempts to eat beauty, to eat what we should only look at. Eve began it. If she caused humanity to be lost by eating the fruit, the opposite attitude, looking at the fruit without eating it, should be what is required to save it." Weil advises that to love others, then, we must pay attention, which consists of "suspending our thought, leaving it detached, empty, and ready to be penetrated by the object." In other words, we must empty ourselves in order to receive the other, to receive the "naked truth." Weil saw Jesus's crucifixion as a model of obedience and attention. It is this attitude that brings about salvation.

In 1943, Weil went to a sanitarium in Kent, England, to recover from pulmonary tuberculosis. While there, she continued to severely restrict her food intake in solidarity with her compatriots in occupied France. At age thirty-four, she died. The death certificate states that the cause of Weil's death was "cardial failure due to myocardial degeneration of the heart muscles due to starvation and pulmonary tuberculosis. The deceased did kill and slay herself by refusing to eat whilst the balance of her mind was disturbed." In other words, the coroner judged her mentally ill and her death a suicide.

Some believe that Weil suffered from anorexia nervosa; but others maintain that while she refrained from eating and was frightfully thin, her concern wasn't with her weight and appearance, nor did she have a distorted view of her body, as do those with anorexia. Weil scholar Alec Irwin says that she understood her "self-imposed food austerities . . . as obedience to God's love." Weil's fasting and restricting were always linked to her hunger for God and her concern for the suffering of the hungry and oppressed.

I learned the stories of other hunger strikers—the suffragettes in England and the United States, the latter led by Alice Paul, who after being arrested for protesting at the White House was force-fed and threatened with commitment to a mental institution; Mohandas Gandhi, in protest of several causes, including British rule of India; labor leader Cesar Chavez, to gain a pay raise for grape pickers and to call attention to the ways in which pesticides were harming farm workers and their families; the more than one hundred Palestinians who took nothing but salt and water for sixty-three days while being held in Israeli prisons, in protest of Israel's use of "administrative detention," the process through which that nation incarcerates Palestinians indefinitely without charge or trial, a violation of international law; and the hunger strikers at Guantanamo Bay, who from 2005 until at least 2013 (when the US military stopped releasing information about the strikes) protested the conditions of their confinement and the long detentions they'd been subjected to without being charged with a crime or brought to trial, persisting in spite of the fact that dozens of them had been strapped down and force-fed through uncomfortably large tubes. For the hunger strikers, controlling something as basic as what does or does not enter their bodies is all they have left. Yet this is no small thing. Using one's body as the arena of sociopolitical protest is one of the highest forms of protest, even if it fails to bring about the desired reform. People have long refrained from eating for spiritual and political reasons. Perhaps those of us with eating disorders or disordered eating are consciously or unconsciously motivated by this tradition.

The seven-year period when the symptoms of my malady subsided was also a time of growing political awareness and activism for me, as well as a time of blossoming artistic expression, a time of yearning, stretching, reaching for and finding God, a time when I sought to grow big. At the same time, I sought to understand why I had tried to make myself small and to live in cramped spaces, why I had tried to satisfy my hungers by starving or restricting or denying them, and why the symptoms of my malady had weakened or abated when I attended to my non-food-related hungers, which coincided with my becoming a mother. In *Waiting for God*, Weil writes,

> The soul knows for certain only that it is hungry. The important thing is that it announces its hunger by crying. A child does not stop crying if we suggest to it that perhaps there is no bread. It goes on crying just the same. The danger is not lest the soul should doubt whether there is any bread, but lest, by a lie, it should persuade itself that it is not hungry.

What I craved and sought to fill myself with was good and real and substantive and nutritious. I would rather have remained hungry than to eat what could never satisfy and was, in fact, mere filler.

CHAPTER EIGHT

FULL

Ian, Meredith, and I are eating dinner at a round, wooden table that seats four. But because our kitchen is so small, we've jammed the table against the wall. To make room for a fourth person would be to sacrifice our precious walking space. The room appears smaller than it is because of the funky burnt-orange, avocado-green, and brown-mushroom wallpaper and the burnt-orange and brown mosaic floor tile, both straight out of the earth-toned 1970s. The woodwork has been painted dark, dark brown. Eventually, Meredith and I will strip the wallpaper, paint the walls a crisp off-white, touch up the woodwork, and cover the floor with cream-colored tile. But for now, the kitchen is busy with outdated patterns.

The food is simple: tortillas with rice, black beans, and salsa for Meredith and me; a pork chop, mashed potatoes, and bread for Ian; a tossed salad for everyone. After I set the food on the table, we pray, thanking God once again for providing our daily bread and for being present at our table, and ask blessings for those who are without. Then we dig in. Belle, our beagle, watches every movement of Ian's fork. Occasionally she snarfs a tidbit that he slips her beneath the table.

As I usually do at family meals, I suggest that we each tell something about our day. This is a composite scene, a blend of the thousands of dinners we've eaten in that kitchen over the eleven years of our lives in that house. But for the sake of simplicity, let's say that the year is 1999. Meredith is eight and in fourth grade; Ian is fifteen and in ninth grade. Meredith's hair is in cornrows, compliments of her stepmother, and she wears glasses, her first pair. She jabbers excitedly about the upcoming science fair. After ruling out her more elaborate proposals that would have required the con-tributions of a hydrologist and a structural engineer, we've decided to do something with water striders and surface tension, though we haven't fig-ured out what. Ian, a husky redhead with very blue eyes and freckled arms, is unbearably excited about his cold-weather Boy Scout campout, still a few weeks away. He attends most of the meetings and participates in the annual fund-raising by selling popcorn door to door as a way to win prizes, but he cares little about earning badges. It's the campouts that he lives for, packing his equipment, then unpacking and repacking it several more times before the day of departure, and poring over Cabela's catalogs, making lists of camping gear he wishes he had. Four days a week, I work at home, teaching in the low-residency master of fine arts program in creative nonfiction of an East Coast college. I rarely tell stories about that part of my life. My story gold mine is the one day each week that I work as a substitute teacher in the Lincoln public schools. I tell about encounters that I had that day with the shop classes, where I knew nothing about the equipment the students were using and they knew it. Our family dinners bear little resemblance to those of the Waltons, with a big, harmonious, extended family gathered around a traditional home-cooked meal. Sometimes the meals at our house are contentious, with Ian and me bickering with each other over schoolwork and house rules. And sometimes the food doesn't turn out very well. But usually we have fun and life feels full when we're gathered there.

If you do a close-up on my face, you'll see that I've gathered wrinkles at the corners of my eyes and creases near my mouth, typical of most women in their early forties. The number 11 is etched between my eyebrows, I wear my long blond hair braided. My jeans are faded. My roomy, baby-blue V-neck sweater is from Goodwill, at this point my favorite little boutique since it's the only place where I can afford to buy clothes. My belly, hips, and thighs are thick and sturdy-looking, though not fat. I'm always saying that if could just lose eight pounds, the baby weight that I never lost fol-lowing my second pregnancy, I'd be content. It doesn't even cross my mind how easily a diet can become the center of one's existence, taking on such force and momentum that it demands complete control and obedience. But I'm not in danger of that happening. I don't diet, can't diet. I stock up at the day-old bread store on the caraway rye bread that I love and sometimes binge on it. Sometimes I bake yeast bread, bagels, or butterhorns or a quick bread like banana or zucchini. Because of my love of sweets, I seldom keep cookies, chocolates, cake, or ice cream in the house. If I bake sweets, it is when I know that Ian and Meredith and perhaps others will be around to eat them. At the meal in this composite scene, I eat two tortillas with the rice and bean filling and salad. Later, when Meredith and I are out walking, we stop by Walgreen's and buy a York Peppermint Patty for her, a Butterfinger for Ian, and a Snickers bar for me.

Meredith's father used to eat at this table, too. In September of 1990, I married Marc, a young, black assistant professor at UNL whom I'd met in a Laundromat during the second year of my doctoral program. He was keenly intelligent, well read, ambitious, extremely self-confident, and magnetic. Because he was West Indian, I found him so not white bread. Ian and I moved into Marc's bachelor house, the little house of the composite scene. Meredith was born on January 11, 1991. My house and life were full—too full, actually. With a family, graduate classes, teaching, and writing, I never had enough time to get anything done the way I wanted it. With only two bedrooms, someone had to sleep in the basement—first Meredith, then Marc and me, and later, Ian. When Marc's youngest sister, Toni, was accepted at UNL and planned to move from New York City to live with us, we moved into a much larger house, with three bedrooms on the second floor and two in the basement, a spacious kitchen, and a hearth room where the round wooden table was too small for the available space, so we put a leaf in it. With the five of us gathered around, eating, joking, and telling stories about our day, life felt complete. When Marc told stories, we laughed so hard that our cheeks and stomachs hurt. We had to plead with him to stop so we could eat.

After five years of marriage, Marc and I divorced. I can say now that the reason our marriage failed had less to do with the fact that we were of different races, cultures, religions, and nations than that we were both rather selfish and we couldn't agree on anything, from money to child-rearing, from the roles of our respective families in our lives to house-cleaning, eating, and sleeping schedules. Since Marc had more personal and financial power than me, his decisions and opinions carried more weight. I often felt frustrated and defeated. Even though I felt some relief that our discordant union was ending, I also felt a deep sadness that this man, who often delighted me and whom I still loved, and I were parting ways. Only five years of marriage—not even enough time to really get acquainted.

After I divorced, I left Lincoln, where I had been a poorly paid instructor at UNL, for a tenure-track position as an assistant professor of English at Southern Illinois University-Carbondale. Ian went with me; Meredith flew back and forth between the Omaha and St. Louis airports, dividing her time between her two homes. In Carbondale, I rented a beautiful old bungalow where our round table fit nicely into the dining room filled with windows and gorgeous woodwork and hardwood floors, its walls covered with a delicate green and white facsimile of an eighteenth-century British chinoiserie wallpaper. My children and I quickly made many friends in our new neighborhood. Even so, it seemed that too much of the time, my home didn't feel full and complete. Each month, I drove four round trips between my home in Carbondale and the St. Louis airport—two hours and twenty minutes each way. The trips to pick up Meredith were joyous; the trips to drop her off were sad. The entire time I lived in Carbondale, I was afraid that Marc would seek and probably win full custody of Meredith since he was the parent who stayed in the same home and the same school district, had more money, and was black. In 1972, the National Association of Black Social Workers stridently opposed transracial adoptions and foster-home placements on the grounds that "only a black family can transmit the emotional and sensitive subtleties of perception and reaction essential for a black child's survival in a racist society," a position that could sway some judges. Even though I wasn't an adoptive or foster parent, I feared that a judge would be more likely to award custody of my biracial daughter to her black father than to her white mother. Being away from Meredith and fearing that I'd lose her in a court battle was my burden and anguish, both waking and sleeping. Though Ian suffered from the lack of a father, I was grateful that I didn't have to fear losing custody of him.

I decided that I'd rather worry about having too little money than about being without my daughter most of the time, so after three years at Southern Illinois University, I resigned from my position and returned to Nebraska so my little family would be together more of the time. When I told Marc my plans, he offered to rent his bachelor house to me, the little house we'd lived in for the first few years of our marriage. Though the little house was too small for the three of us, Marc gave me a good deal on the rent and I knew he would maintain the property. It seemed right for us to be returning to our old, familiar neighborhood, where so many of our former neighbors still lived. On July 22, 1998, we moved in.

It wasn't "normal" life that we lived in our new-old house. Ian lived with me all the time; Meredith continued to go "back and forth," as she called it—though now just across the city rather than three states. She alternated between two days at my house and two days at her dad's, over and over, from second grade until she graduated from high school. Even when she spent her summers at home during college, we maintained this schedule that we'd all grown accustomed to. In a sense, I, too, went back and forth between life with Ian and Meredith and life with Ian, between a house that was full and one that was almost full. When Meredith was with me, I tried to make up for lost time. We played music together, Meredith on her violin and me on my flute; we read, did homework, or watched television together, or took long rambles through our part of the city. Because Ian was there every day, I didn't feel the same pressure to spend undivided time with him. He and I had more spontaneous and fewer planned times together.

When we returned to the little house, Ian was thirteen, an age at which he was just as happy to cook his own food. And, too, he wanted meat, while Meredith and I ate vegetarian meals. One of Meredith's and my favorite meals was homemade pizza with plenty of black olives, onions, and weird toppings—sauerkraut, chopped broccoli, eggplant, or lamb's quarters, the last harvested from the backyard. We'd go heavy on the tomato sauce, but since neither of us cared much for cheese, we'd leave it off. Ian said he'd rather eat a frozen cardboard pizza with artificial cheese than one of our weird concoctions. For the three of us to eat a meal together, I had to plan something "normal" like spaghetti or lasagna. Otherwise, I cooked one meal for Meredith and me and one for Ian.

In so many ways, my life was anything but white bread. Essentially, my son had no father. I married a black man and our daughter is biracial—commonplace now but not in 1991. I studied yoga for a couple of decades before it became mainstream, and I taught it for a while. I earned a master's degree and a PhD in English, not for the job prospects, which were limited, but simply because I loved studying literature and writing. The white-bread choice would have been to go into a field with better opportunities and more pay—medicine, law, engineering, business, actuarial science, computer programming. After three years at Southern Illinois University, I was asked to go up for early tenure. The white-bread choice would have been to seek the promotion, with a pay raise and lifelong job security, move into a bigger, fancier house, save money for college educations and retirement, and buy more stuff, more geegaws. Instead, I resigned from my position and moved back to Nebraska, where I lived in a state of what I think of as genteel poverty. I've yet to meet anyone else who has walked away from a position at the same time they became a likely candidate for early tenure.

What made it possible for me to move back to Lincoln was that I'd been offered a good part-time position teaching in the low-residency Master of Fine Arts Program in Creative Nonfiction at Goucher College in Baltimore, Maryland, a job that required me to be on campus for two weeks every summer and to work from wherever I wanted the rest of the year reading my students' manuscripts and conferencing with them about their projects. This job paid my utilities and rent and, after I bought the little house, my mortgage. To pick up gas and grocery money and to cover unexpected expenses, I was a substitute teacher in the public schools, took a few private writing students, and sold my writing whenever I could. Even so, when I told one friend my annual income, she gasped. "No one can live on that little," she said. Though my family never had quite enough in material terms, neither were we ever completely without. To live within our means, we did without cable TV, machine-dried clothes, credit card debt, short trips in the car, garbage service, newspaper and magazine subscriptions, restaurant and convenience foods, or a retirement plan for me. Ian was covered by Medicaid and Meredith by her father's health insurance, but I had a practically worthless commercial policy with a $10,000 deductible. I was comfortable saying no to many of the excesses of our culture and was a bit evangelical in telling people what it was possible to do without. In my wallet, I carried a slip of paper with a quotation (edited so that it's gender neutral) by Henry David Thoreau that inspired me: "A person is rich in proportion to the number of things which she or he can afford to let alone."

Ian and Meredith had very different childhoods. Ian was doubly deprived because his father was not only negligent but absent. On the rare occasion that Gerald called or visited, it was usually hurtful and negative. Since I had only my income to support Ian, he also suffered from the lack of money, as children do in this money-worshipping culture. This is one of my deepest and most enduring regrets: that Ian was acutely aware that the material comfort and security taken for granted by so many of the children that he knew at school, church, and Boy Scouts wasn't his. Meredith's father was a strong and steady presence in her life, paying his share and often, part of mine. Meredith benefited enormously from what two devoted parents and enough well-spent money can do for a child and emerged with a strong sense of self-esteem and, because of the financial hardships that she sometimes experienced at my house, a strong sense of social justice.

Time was and continues to be my pearl of great price. I gave up the more than adequate income of a tenure-track position so I could tend to my children. If I'd had a conventional job, my children would have had to do without many things—like all the chauffeuring I did. I drove Meredith to school, violin lessons, other music events, swimming, debate, ballet, and, later, volunteer work and part-time jobs, and I made sure that she was present for every rehearsal of the Lincoln Junior Youth Orchestra and the Lincoln Youth Symphony. As she became a more committed, accomplished, and in-demand violinist, the time investment for both of us increased considerably. I drove Ian to school, Boy Scouts, Civil Air Patrol, church youth group activities, and part-time jobs. When he was in high school, he hooked up with a bad crowd. Then I drove him to appointments with counselors, diversion officers, and court-ordered community service. When a juvenile court judge sent Ian to a boys' reformatory a hundred miles away, I drove to visit him every Saturday for four months, taking with me newspapers, board games, toiletries, home-cooked meals (much to my surprise and delight, most of them actually looked and tasted good), and once, his beagle. During this time, I woke up every morning with a clear sense of purpose: my children needed me. Sometimes I doubted that I had the sheer energy, discipline, and selflessness to be at once breadwinner, parent, teacher, writer, and keeper of the hearth. Usually, though, I was too busy to dwell on this and simply did what had to be done.

But I failed my children in the kitchen. They do not have warm and fuzzy memories of my cooking—like those I have about my mother's butterhorn rolls, bread-and-butter pickles, fudge, coleslaw, catsupy meatloaf, fried catfish, and lattice-topped fruit or meringue-topped cream pies. My children will never rave about my cooking or my ability to nurture them and others with food, though I suspect they'll marvel at the fact that somehow, they survived my kitchen disasters and they'll have some good laughs at my expense about limp vegetables, jaw-breaking stuffing, muffins with burnt bottoms, weird substitutions (catsup and salsa to make up for not enough jarred spaghetti sauce), birthday layer cakes held together with toothpicks, the whole sloping mess disguised under an avalanche of frosting, soupy fudge (part of a Christmas gift for each of Meredith's teachers), and all those church potlucks where I left with most of the salad that I'd contributed to the meal still in the serving bowl. I tell them that the two summers I spent cooking in a nursing-home kitchen when I was eighteen and nineteen ruined my culinary abilities. Bland and overcooked is what I was trained to do. But, too, I suspect that my conflicted relationship with food contributed to this sorry state of affairs.

Early in my marriage, I tried to cook. Dinners. Every evening. All by myself. But there was just too much to balance. Meredith was the easy one: she ate what I ate. I was trying to raise Ian as a vegetarian, like me, but when he entered school and when I married, two events that coincided, he campaigned hard to become an omnivore. I compromised. He could be an omnivore at school and a vegetarian at home. But eventually I saw that vegetarianism was a strain for him, so I let him make his own food choices. My West Indian husband had fond memories of dishes and ingredients that I'd never heard of, much less knew how to make—pepper pot, curry and roti, curry ghanna, swordfish, red cake, black cake, and mari-wiri peppers. What could I cook that everyone would eat? And with two children to take care of, a dissertation to write, and classes to teach, how would I find the time?

The story of one of the foods I made for my family, a simple quiche made of eggs, cream, diced chicken, cheese, green onions, and seasonings, stands as an emblematic tale about my attitude toward cooking. I'd never (and still haven't) made a good pie crust, so I bought one from the freezer case at the grocery. In place of real chicken, I used Worthington Diced Chik, made from textured vegetable protein. But everything else, I measured, chopped, and mixed just as the recipe said to and baked it the exact amount of time required. I also baked potatoes and boiled broccoli to accompany it. Voilà! A decent, edible meal. Ian was happy because he liked eggs and the quiche contained something that looked and tasted like meat. Marc liked it because the quiche had a nice texture and flavor. I was happy because everyone ate it. The meal was such a hit that it became a once-a-week standard. But each week, I became a little laxer in my adherence to the recipe. After all, what was a recipe but a suggestion or a set of instructions meant to be interpreted or personalized? Not enough eggs? Just add more diced onion. Nobody will notice that the quiche isn't as light and airy as the original. No cream? Hmm. Just add the liquid in which the diced chicken was packed. My family poured that quiche onto the potatoes as a topping. Every quiche I made was so unlike the others that one evening when everyone was seated at the table awaiting the next permutation, Marc asked, "Will this quiche be a solid, liquid, or gas?"

Finally, Marc told me that my cooking was absolutely awful. I was hurt, but not surprised. "Cooking takes time," he said. "If you just throw things together, that's how it's going to taste." That's what I didn't want to do: waste a lot of time making something look and taste good that would be so quickly consumed. Instead of planning or preparing meals, I'd rather read or write or take a walk or a nap or have sex or watch a movie. Food was fuel and fuel was energy. Simple food did the job as well as more complex and demanding dishes.

Ian was thrilled when his stepfather took over a good share of the cooking. Baked red snapper. Oxtail soup with chunks of sweet potato floating in the broth. Sauteed garbanzo beans and onions. Pepper pot. Okra stew. Salt fish. Barbecued ribs. And chicken—curried, barbecued, or cubed in chow mein. Marc like his food hot enough that he'd break a sweat as he ate. In fact, the curry he used was so hot that he kept the can on a high shelf in the cupboard, out of the children's reach.

After my sister-in-law Toni moved in, she made West Indian cook-up rice with chunks of beef stew meat, black-eyed peas, tomatoes, onions, coconut milk, and an almost intolerable amount of black pepper. I scooped out the rice and beans and pretended that they hadn't cooked in the same pot as the meat. Some rules *are* meant to be bent. We ate cook-up for supper, breakfast, and, if there was any left, lunch, and divvied up the coveted "bun-bun," the burnt chunks that stuck to the bottom of the pot. I cooked, too, making vegetarian spaghetti, lasagna, chow mein, okra stew, chili, and of course my specialty, quiche. When I only had to cook a couple of times a week, the meals that I served turned out far better than when cooking was a daily obligation.

I learned quite a few things about cooking from Marc. I'd never eaten a sweet potato that wasn't candied or served as a side dish. But now I rarely make a soup that doesn't include one or more. I developed a taste for spicier foods, especially if the heat came from a high quality curry or black pepper. And I learned that I don't have to like to cook.

For twenty-seven years, my home was full. The filling began late in 1983, not with Ian's birth, but with his conception and his growing presence, and it ended during the spring of 2011, the year before Meredith moved away to New York City. Ian left home in stages, moving out several times and into other abodes with his long-time girlfriend before finally and completely in 2007, when I sold my little house. Following his final move out, Ian asked if we could have Sunday dinners together at my house. Of course, I answered yes. Sometimes I cooked for him and his girlfriend, but more often, I picked up something already prepared and well made. Meredith graduated from high school in 2008. Instead of going to a private, out-of-state school, as she had dreamed, she went to UNL, our hometown university, on a regent's scholarship. Even though she wasn't far in terms of physical distance, living in a dorm for two years and a duplex within walking distance of the university for two more, and though she spent a Saturday or Sunday afternoon with me each weekend, doing laundry, grocery shopping, cooking, eating, and talking, the slow, gradual work of severing was hard and sad. The coup de grâce came not in August of 2012, when she moved to Manhattan for graduate school and a professional life beyond graduation, but the conclusion of her junior year of college, when I began the awful countdown to her day of departure.

For two decades, I was free of my malady. I ate with gusto at potlucks, in restaurants, at other people's houses, and in my own home. I did not go to bed hungry. I did not hide food in my clothes closet or throw it away because it might be tainted. I did not let the number on the scale determine my mood for the day. I did not think about food every minute. I did not believe that by restricting my eating I could tame my unruly body and appetites or protect myself from sorrow or pain. For two decades, I was healthy.

If, during that time, I had been asked to tell the story of my life, I wouldn't have mentioned my malady because that experience felt so far away and I had changed enough (or so I believed) that it would never happen to me again. The deep story of my remission is that by no longer obsessing about eating, food, and weight, I had the time, energy, and attention for other things. I married and divorced, raised children, earned graduate degrees, learned and practiced a profession and an art, and kept my family and home together as a single-income single parent—a formidable labor of love. I had little desire for a social life outside of what my children and their various activities provided. I was still the same person I always had been, introverted, perfectionistic, cautious, lacking in confidence, prone to worry and pessimism. But motherhood called me to be a better person than I would have been if I'd only had myself to answer to, and so I was also hopeful, courageous, responsible, and more self-sacrificing than I thought possible.

During the twenty years when I was free of my disordered eating, I built upon the changes in my personal and professional life that had begun during the seven-year period of transition that preceded it. I was still searching for—and finding—God, still searching for social justice, still searching for ways to write essays that mattered, and I was striving to raise children who would have rich and fulfilling lives. I was always aware that my son and daughter were leaving me, little by little. At any moment during their childhoods, I could have told you the number of years and months that remained before each would graduate from high school and move on to something else. I couldn't imagine then what awaited me after they left and how I would have to find new ways to love them through separation and distance.

CHAPTER NINE

THE GRIEVING SEASON

In June of 2011, when I was fifty-four, I drove from my home in Lincoln to an environmental literature conference at Indiana University Blooming-ton. It was an epic journey, made even longer because the record flooding on the Missouri and Mississippi Rivers required long detours that added several hours to the trip each way. On the way to and from the conference, I stopped at Carbondale to visit dear friends that I'd known since I was an as-sistant professor in the English Department at Southern Illinois University during the mid-1990s. I was eager to see my old buddies and colleagues in Carbondale and at the conference, and since I had just months earlier com-pleted a book about rivers, I was also looking forward to seeing the rivers I'd written about and to meet some new ones.

Packing for this trip was tricky. Because of a gastrointestinal condition and a food sensitivity, I brought with me almost all the food that I would eat on the trip: organic apples, gluten-free oatmeal with brown sugar, fresh pineapple, and rice cakes. During the four days that I was at the conference, I ate three restaurant meals—a small salad at a café, curried vegetables at an Indian restaurant, and a cup of good butternut squash soup from a little soup counter near the hotel. Most of my other meals came from my stash. When I ran out of pineapple, I'd go by a grocery store and pay a deli worker to cut a whole one into peeled chunks. I drank two cups of green tea in the morning and one in the afternoon. The rest of the time, I drank herbal tea and once, juice. In Carbondale, I picked at evening meals at the homes of two of my friends, meals I couldn't avoid without appearing rude. I felt uneasy and apologetic as I questioned my hosts about the food ingredients and preparations but then nibbled only little bits of it. How different I must have seemed to my friends and colleagues, in whose company I'd once eaten with relish and with no reservations at potlucks, at picnics, in restaurants, and at each other's homes. I explained about my health condition and the regrettable limitations it imposed. So sorry that I can't eat the pesto and cheesecake, but boy is this salad delicious. Except for the nights when I had dinner at my friends' houses, I went to bed with an empty stomach every night during this trip. For several months prior to my trip, I'd been eating less and less and would continue to eat less than I needed for many months after I returned. The restricting that I did on this trip was no different than what I'd been doing at home. But because of the eventfulness of this journey and the social aspect of it, I remember the details clearly.

One evening before I stepped into the shower at the conference hotel, I stood in front of the bathroom mirrors—a three-way over the sink and a full-length mirror on the door—and scrutinized my naked body and my face. The lighting there was much better than in my bathroom at home, and the combination of mirrors allowed me to see myself from all angles. Of course, I felt the shock that most if not all older women feel when they behold reflections of their bare bodies. The image in the mirror was so at odds with the image of myself that I carry in my head and with my "felt" age, which shifts according to circumstances, though usually I think of myself as being in my early forties. But I was in for another shock. At that point, I'd lost about seventeen pounds or so from my almost five-foot two-inch frame—the first time I'd lost weight since my twenties. My face looked slacker and longer than it had before my weight loss. My clavicles were prominent; each shoulder was capped by a bony point. My ribs, visible from my armpits to my waist and from my clavicles to my sternum, reminded me of a washboard. I looked over my shoulder and saw a string of knobs, my spine. Prominent veins stood out on my arms and abdomen. My breasts, always small, were even tinier, and both the grape-sized lumps and the gritty little knots on the outer sides that I used to be able to find only with my fingertips, I could now see in the mirror. My thighs were separated by an oval-ish space; my calves, always so fleshy that it was all but impossible for me to find boots that fit, now seemed normal sized, which made my knees look larger. I liked the way that I appeared in my clothes now that I was thinner, but when naked under bright lights, I looked older and more withered than I had just months earlier, when I was fleshier and my skin tighter and smoother. I was delighted by my thinness yet frightened by the exposure of my underlying structure. How easy, now, to imagine myself as a fleshless, hairless skeleton.

I remember another motel bathroom. During my first bout with my malady, when I was fifteen and lost 22 percent of my body weight in just a few months, my family went on a road trip. Before I stepped into the shower one day, I looked at myself carefully in the motel bathroom mirror. My saddlebags were almost gone, which thrilled me, but what struck me was that I could see the branching blue veins on my torso that previously had been hidden beneath layers of fat. Seeing my underlying structure was fascinating and frightening. I didn't realize how much my body had changed until that moment.

My two road trips, thirty-nine years apart, were similar in another way. On that earlier trip, when my family picnicked or stopped for fast food, I ate the fruit and puffed-rice cereal that I'd brought from home instead of joining them for Kentucky Fried Chicken and the fixings or burgers and fries. When we went to sit-down restaurants, I ordered iceberg lettuce salads and "no-cal" dressing or a side order of cooked cabbage, green beans, or a plain baked potato (no butter, please!). And I drank a lot of caffeinated diet pop. As I, a woman in my mid-fifties, gazed at my reflection in the hotel mirror, I didn't fully grasp that what had happened to me when I was fifteen was happening again.

Severely restricting at fifteen and again in my mid-twenties doesn't strike me as out of the ordinary in a skin-deep culture that bases so much of a person's worth on material possessions and physical appearance, with thinness being the epitome of beauty for women. But restricting again at fifty-four does. After all, I had accomplished so much. I was the mother of an adult son and daughter; a prolific and award-winning author of four books, with a fifth, my river book, which would win a state and an international writing award, just accepted for publication; an associate professor of English at a state university; a church-committee member; a homeowner; a political activist; and a contributor to various worthy charities. Most significantly, I had decades of psychotherapy behind me with a series of therapists ranging from adequate to brilliant, and I'd read widely about the causes of eating disorders and disordered eating. I preferred depth and substance over surface and fluff, so I watched little television outside of PBS and C-SPAN, read books with challenging ideas, saw films instead of movies, and had friends with whom I had more absorbing and consequential matters to discuss (like the life of the mind and the state of our souls) than the size of our butts. But at fifty-four, three years into menopause, I once again felt the shift and heard the click that accompanied both of my earlier episodes of severe restricting and substantial weight loss. The shift and the click moved me into a higher gear, where I felt full and triumphant in proportion to how little I consumed, where I conquered my unruly body and appetites, where through my easy denial, I was proving something to someone, though I couldn't say what or to whom. For a brief moment in front of the mirror in the Hilton Garden Inn in Bloomington, Indiana, I lightly, briefly acknowledged what I had chosen not to see, and it scared me. But it didn't send me to the streets for an ice cream sundae or a cheesy burrito, nor did it stop me from recording and tallying every calorie I was consuming. When I returned home, what I'd seen in the mirror and what it meant faded from my awareness. I would have argued with anyone who tried to tell me that I was eating less than is required to sustain my bodily processes or that something in my life and my thinking was faulty and out of control. Because of my denial, I would continue restricting and drop about thirteen more pounds. Then I would look even more wizened and aged than I had in the hotel mirror—the very things that I feared.

When I returned from my epic journey in the summer of 2011, I told my twenty-year-old daughter how frustrated I was that in spite of all the dietary and lifestyle changes I had made to try to improve my gastrointestinal condition, I had not gotten relief. Meredith knew fragments of the story of my long and conflicted history with food. "You have an eating disorder," she said in a firm and motherly tone of voice. "If you don't start eating more, you're going to die." During her junior year of college, Meredith had dieted and trained for a full marathon, replacing her roundness with angles. Since then, she had tried various diets, including intermittent fasting and the Whole30 Program. She understood how easily a health regimen could become a preoccupation or a consuming obsession. She is insightful, frank, and only wants the best for me. Her words shook me. I thought of the similar images that I'd seen in the bathroom mirrors in two different motels separated by thirty-nine years—images that were equal in their ability to disturb and exhilarate—and my brief acknowledgment of what they meant. I knew in a way what could no longer be denied or forgotten: that once again, I was trying to become just a whisper, a shadow, a flicker.

During this time of stringent, inflexible restricting, in 2011 and 2012, I would have told you that I wasn't dieting to lose weight. Rather, I had a food sensitivity and a gastrointestinal problem and had to carefully monitor what and when I ate. My weight loss was a product of my best efforts to make myself healthy.

The gastrointestinal condition had begun about a year earlier. Many times each day, enough sticky phlegm or thick saliva rose in my throat that I felt gurgly. Coughing couldn't dislodge the blockage, though aggressively and repeatedly clearing my throat sometimes brought relief. On several occasions, the mucus lodged in my trachea and I stopped breathing. When this happened in the presence of others, I did a wild pantomime until someone pounded on my back or shook me until the obstruction broke loose. When this happened when I was alone, I was eventually able to clear the clog, apparently through good luck and panicky movements. But would this work every time?

Fear of suffocation led me to consult with my general practitioner, who said that my symptoms were caused by gastroesophageal reflux disease (GERD). The phlegm that sometimes stole my breath was my body's attempt to protect my esophagus from irritation when the contents of my stomach backed up into my food tube. Since the delicate lining of the esophagus can't tolerate gastric acid the way the stomach can, prolonged exposure can cause bleeding ulcers, inflammation, and scarring of the esophageal lining, which make breathing and swallowing difficult. Erosion of the lining is of particular concern since it can lead to Barrett's esophagus, a condition in which the normal cells that line the lower part of the esophagus are replaced by intestinal cells. People with Barrett's are at a higher risk than those without it of developing esophageal cancer, one of the deadliest cancers. Author and philosopher Christopher Hitchens was diagnosed with esophageal cancer, the same cancer that had killed his father, in June of 2010. He died nineteen months later, but not before he wrote about the difficulties of trying to write with chemo brain, about losing his voice, about facing his own death, and about being "thin at last." I was scared.

An endoscopy of my upper GI tract revealed that my lower esophageal sphincter (LES), the ring of muscle between the lower esophagus and the stomach, was weak. Because the common pharmaceutical solutions to decrease the production of gastric acid didn't work for me, my doctor said that I might be a good candidate for Nissen fundoplication, a procedure in which a surgeon strengthens the LES by wrapping the fundus, the upper curve of the stomach, around the valve and sewing it into place, so that acid can't as easily back up into the esophagus. From my research, I knew that this was a controversial surgery with troubling side effects, such as the inability to burp or vomit. Surgery, I decided, would be my last resort.

In the meantime, I took matters into my own hands. I tried several natural remedies, including bromelain, a strongly neutralizing enzyme found in fresh pineapple; raw, organic apple cider vinegar, which hastens the digestion of fats; wild marshmallow root, which has slippery, coating properties; sodium alginic acid, a seaweed extract, which forms a viscous barrier between the gastric contents of the stomach and the esophagus. I adopted a high-alkaline, low-acid diet, which called for the elimination of most grains, fats, sugars, and animal products, including dairy. Some of these efforts helped a little. But none helped very much. I worked with two practitioners of traditional Chinese medicine, both of whom stuck long needles in me, which felt surprisingly good. One of the practitioners said that my problem was "rebellious Chi" since my vital energy wanted to go up instead of down. At talk therapy, I explored the metaphorical nature of fire in the belly, my rebellious vital energy, blockage in the throat, and my inability to let go of what I'd been chewing on and let it pass. I mentioned that I had a history of disordered eating, but that had been long ago. Surely it had nothing to do with my current ailment.

At the same time, I altered the way I did almost everything so that my esophagus was always higher than my stomach. I jacked up the head of my bed and slept on a slope. I ate smaller and more frequent meals so that my stomach was never full. I ate nothing in the evening, drank nothing after eight o'clock. In 1998, I had been diagnosed with gluten sensitivity. Many times since then, I'd gone on and off a gluten-free diet. But in 2011, I was so uncomfortable after eating a piece of cake at a university event that I swore off gluten for good—a vow that I've kept. I continued to eat the curries and chilies that I love since spicy foods created no more distress than bland ones. I stopped leaping upstairs, bending over to pull weeds, running, dancing, or jumping for joy since these movements could cause acid to rise in my esophagus, and I stopped practicing any yoga asana that put my esophagus level with or lower than my stomach.

Because of the dietary changes I was making, my weight dropped to a number that I hadn't seen since middle school. While this delighted me and while the new dietary restrictions and lifestyle changes I imposed upon myself made me feel in charge and therefore safer, I was frustrated that they weren't curing or even lessening the severity or frequency of the obstruction in my throat. In response, I made my rules even tighter—instead of not eating within three hours of going to bed, I moved my dinnertime back four and then five hours. I figured that if I ate smaller meals or, better yet, skipped meals, there'd be less food, less gastric acid in my stomach to back up into my esophagus. But the more I tried to create balance in my digestive tract, the more out of balance my life became. Despite my changes and my doctor's efforts to find a medication that I could tolerate, phlegm continued to clog my throat and steal my peace. The thought never occurred to me that if nothing was helping, including going to bed with a stomach rolling with hunger pangs, why not give up and go out for a night of pizza, beer, and wild, fast dancing?

Two doctors, one a specialist, had diagnosed my ailment as GERD, and I believed them. But I also knew that there was more to my condition than just that. I referred myself to the University of Nebraska Medical Center in Omaha, where tests revealed that, much to my surprise, I was refluxing very little. The cause of my throat and breathing problems, the doctor there said, was an esophageal motility disorder. Instead of a smooth and coordinated wave of contractions down the lower esophagus when I swallowed, my muscles alternated between this normal peristalsis and simultaneous contractions, the latter of which worked against the easy passage of food and liquid. It was saliva, the GI doctor explained, not phlegm, that was pooling in my esophagus and making it hard to clear my throat and occasionally taking my breath. While it's not clear what causes the spasms, they appear to be related to abnormal functioning of the nerves that control the smooth muscles in the lower esophagus.

The GI professor recommended a calcium channel blocker or an antianxiety drug to relax the smooth muscles of my esophagus. If that didn't solve the problem, he said that he could stretch my esophagus with a balloon. I was relieved by the diagnosis, yet concerned by the chemical treatments he was recommending. If my condition was as exquisitely responsive to stress and anxiety as the doctor said it was, the right prescription, I thought, was for me to figure out why I was holding tension and then find ways to release it or, better yet, to keep it from developing. It seemed to me that intensive journaling, a deeper yoga practice, and frequent acts of surrender were the right remedy.

While I was disturbed and at times indignant that I had lived with a wrong and expensive diagnosis for over a year and that I'd suffered in ways I shouldn't have had to, and though I was deeply troubled by the fact that I had been asked to consider a surgery that might not have alleviated my symptoms and, worse, might have created others that were just as dangerous, I was also concerned about this new diagnosis since my symptoms didn't match several of those the doctor listed. For instance, I didn't have chest pain or difficulty swallowing. Could this diagnosis also be wrong? Yet my joy and relief were greater that I didn't have GERD. I also felt empowered by the fact that I had listened to my intuition and sought a third opinion.

As soon as I received the new diagnosis, my choking symptoms began abating, which made me a little more relaxed about what I ate and when. I stuck the prescription for the calcium channel blocker to my refrigerator door with a magnet in case I needed to fill it. But I never did. As a precaution, I continued eating small, frequent meals from the same limited list of choices, though I ate my last meal of the day at a more normal time. I felt uneasy and suspicious about something in this situation that I couldn't identify or name. Why had my choking symptoms immediately and almost completely disappeared after I received the new diagnosis? If I was "cured," why was I continuing to restrict my eating, though to a less severe degree than I had been? Why was it easier to be hungry than full, to have such a narrow list of "acceptable" foods, to never ever be tempted by cookies, cake, pasta, bread? Why did I feel so much dread when I received a dinner invitation or when my students brought food to share with the class that I looked for ways to get out of participating? Why was I weighing myself so many times each day and allowing the number in the little window on the scale to determine my mood? Could an eating disorder, which my daughter insisted is what I had, be connected to my symptoms and my fear and sadness?

Perhaps I had unconsciously created the symptoms of a condition that gave me an excuse to eat so little. Perhaps I had created a condition that allowed me to speak to myself through my body rather than through words and ideas. If so, how far could I push the metaphorical nature of my digestive condition? I remember chewing and spitting, something I started during the Punishing Summer. I'd put food into my mouth and chew, but refuse to swallow the masticated food, refuse to incorporate the nourishment and calories it contained into my body. What was it now, I wondered, that I found so hard to swallow?

I did what I always do when I don't have the answers I need: I researched and wrote about it. I read the results of recent studies about eating disorders and disordered eating in medical journals, as well as articles for laypeople in the *Guardian,* the *New York Times, Forbes* magazine, the *Huffington Post,* and other publications. I browsed through websites and blogs where the eating disordered, their loved ones, and those who treat them communicate their stories and opinions with varying levels of proficiency and knowledge. I was surprised to learn that more older women than ever before are seeking treatment for their eating disorders and disordered eating and speaking out about their conditions. What I was experiencing wasn't unusual.

Most experts agree that about 10 percent of those with eating disorders are older women, though the percentage may be higher. Yet researcher Cynthia Bulik says that because older women with eating disorders disguise or misread their symptoms as being due to a health condition such as a digestive problem, food sensitivities, or changes associated with aging, many aren't included in the number of reported eating disorders. Ninety percent of people who are restricting, binging, or purging don't receive treatment. The reasons for this are various. Among the 90 percent are those with "subclinical," "threshold," "borderline," or "almost" anorexia, many of whom are placed in the "other specified feeding or eating disorder" category, which means that their symptoms don't meet the narrow diagnostic criteria for full-syndrome anorexia nervosa, bulimia nervosa, or binge-eating disorder and so might not be taken seriously by themselves or others. Though some with eating disorders and disordered eating are able to hold down jobs and care for their families, they can still suffer from the physical and psychological symptoms of their disorder.

In fact, in *Almost Anorexic: Is My (or My Loved One's) Relationship with Food a Problem?*, Jennifer Thomas and Jenni Schaefer say that some studies show there is no difference in the mortality rates of full-blown and subclinical anorexia. The 90 percent also includes those who don't connect their symptoms, such as their paralyzing self-consciousness and perfectionism or eating so little yet thinking about food all the time, with a disease that "only teenagers get"; those who don't see anything abnormal about their food-related behaviors in a culture where so many "normal" people are dieting or overeating; those who would agree to inpatient or outpatient treatment if they could afford it or if their insurance policies covered it (according to a recent estimate by the Aetna Insurance Company, inpatient treatment ranges from $500 to $2,000 a day, with patients needing from three to six months of care); those who can't leave work and family for weeks at a time or who live too far from a clinic or specialist to take advantage of outpatient treatment; those who can't "come out" with their condition because it would compromise their status or position; and those who are conflicted about or dead set against giving up their old friend and foe, their sword and shield against danger and pain, and getting well.

But perhaps the most important reasons we do not seek treatment are that we think we can handle it ourselves and there is no one pushing us to do otherwise. A fifty-something woman doesn't have parents watching and worrying over her behaviors or coaxing her to talk to the therapist or to enter treatment, as a teenager does, so she isn't among those counted as having an eating disorder or severe enough disordered eating that it should be treated. Also, a smart older woman can be very clever. She can conceal, camouflage, or explain away those behaviors that would reveal her disease by lying or joshing about what she has or hasn't eaten, by pushing food around on her plate, by slipping it into the garbage when no one is looking, by giving it to others so she doesn't have to eat it, or, in restaurants, by giving painstakingly explicit directions about food preparation (no fish oil, no MSG, no mushrooms, sauce on the side) and then not eating her meal because she swears that that little tan speck is part of a mushroom, which surely will cause anaphylactic shock. If she lives alone, she doesn't have to conceal her strange eating rituals when at home. Unlike teenagers, she can walk into a drugstore and buy all the laxatives, diuretics, and emetics she wants without raising suspicions. A smart older woman can defend the physical and psychological benefits of many hours spent exercising each day even if that commitment interferes with a normal social life and feels more punitive than fun or restorative. A smart older woman can claim quite convincingly that her zealous adherence to the Mediterranean or Ayurvedic or anti-inflammatory or Ornish or gluten-free or Paleo or anti-candida or alkaline or Bulletproof diet is actually making her healthier, as she further and further limits the list of foods acceptable for her consumption until there is little left that isn't forbidden.

Not all older women who have these thoughts and display these actions have anorexia or almost anorexia. Some have orthorexia nervosa. Derived from the Greek words for "correct" or "right" (*orthos*) and "appetite" (*orexis*), *orthorexia* literally means "correct appetite." This condition involves an obsession with eating only those foods that the orthorectic considers pure or healthful or safe. In *Health Food Junkies: Orthorexia Nervosa: Overcoming the Obsession with Healthful Eating,* Steven Bratman, the physician who coined the term in 1997, and David Knight point out that while an anorectic wants to lose weight, an orthorectic wants to feel pure, healthy, and natural. Because of these concerns, the orthorectic may gradually restrict herself to a diet of raw organic vegetables and one tablespoon per day of organic, extra virgin olive oil or a diet free of artificial colors, flavors, preservatives, and GMOs. Even though orthorexia is not listed in the latest edition of the American Psychiatric Association's *Diagnostic and Statistical Manual* along with other officially recognized eating disorders, such as anorexia nervosa, bulimia nervosa, and binge-eating disorder, it is a prevalent condition. I see the symptoms—fretting over food, keeping to such a restrictive diet that one can't eat anywhere but at home, ritualizing one's food-related behaviors, and refusing to eat foods one deems impure, polluted, tamasic, unwholesome, adulterated, inferior, tainted, toxic, or lacking in vitality—in several women I know, as well as in myself. As the orthorectic becomes increasingly rigid and restrictive, her disease can easily tip over into anorexia, which takes on a life of its own, refusing to let anything else run the show. I handle my own restrictions by only eating at home or, if I go out, only eating under certain circumstances. I am so scrupulously faithful in following my healthful diet (oatmeal and nuts for breakfast, stir-fried vegetables for lunch, fruit with either frozen yogurt or a protein bar for dinner, rice cakes for snacks) that my caloric consumption rarely deviates by more than fifty calories per day, and I never, ever binge or splurge. Does that make me one with orthorexia or with subthreshold anorexia? A blend of the two? Something else? Does the name even matter if the end result is the same?

Experts and nonexperts alike offer similar and equally facile explanations as to why women in their forties, fifties, sixties, and beyond are self-starving, as they do with fifteen- or twenty-year-olds. A chief executive of a British charitable organization devoted to helping those with eating disorders said that the increasing number of middle-aged women seeking help for anorexia is partly due to the "*Desperate Housewives* syndrome." Until recently, women over forty weren't featured in magazines. But now, when ordinary women behold images of the "fabulous and flawless" likes of Madonna, Sharon Stone, Teri Hatcher, Salma Hayek, or Julianne Moore, they feel like failures. And so they take charge of their eating. Unfortunately, those images *are* influential. But the expert's analysis fails since she doesn't ask *why* bag-of-bones Gwyneth Paltrow and Michelle Pfeiffer are considered worthy of emulation in this time and place when for most of human history, full faces, round bellies, and large, fleshy hips and breasts were the ideal and the crumpling and creasing of the face and bending of the spine that come with age were associated with the honorable accumulation of experience and knowledge.

Another expert, a professor in a department of psychiatry at a Canadian university, says that older women restrict because of what she calls "some visible physical stigmata of aging." *Stigmata*, according to the dictionary, are "mark[s] of disgrace or infamy" or "mental or physical mark[s] that [are] characteristic of a defect or disease." Defects or disgraces such as wrinkled skin, sagging breasts and buttocks, bat wings, a bulging belly, and decreasing muscle mass. According to this view, because of the twelve pounds that the average woman gains within twelve years of menopause, and because of dropping estrogen levels that result in shifts in fat distribution that cause "midriff bulge," older women are so dissatisfied with their bodies in a culture that vigorously and persistently exalts youth and thinness that they restrict or binge and purge. While this is true, again I ask, why is it now shameful for a postmenopausal woman to weigh more than a younger woman? And why do we look to young women and teenagers, even, as the reference point for physical beauty? If our culture revered the sagacity, discernment, and patience that come with age, a typical post-menopausal weight gain would be seen as beautiful and desirous and we'd look forward to the day when we, too, would be thick, gray, wrinkled, and treasured for what we could teach others about living and loving well.

Let's say that those people are right who believe that we older women who restrict or binge and purge are primarily driven by the desire to look young and thin so that people will approve of and love us. I would be mightily disappointed in the results. After I lost over one-fifth of my body weight in the course of a year, only eight people said anything to me about it: my mother; my daughter; two colleagues, both about fifteen years older than me; a student of mine who is my age; two people at church; and an old friend, also a few years older than me. None of these people told me I looked good or better. Since such weight loss can be a sign of disease, it's especially troubling that only three in this small group asked about my health. People who did *not* notice my weight loss include the general practitioner I'd gone to for nineteen years, the gynecologist I'd gone to for sixteen years, and the gastroenterologist I'd seen several times. Yet at each appointment in these three offices, a nurse told me to step on the scale and recorded my weight. Others who didn't notice include all but two people at the church I'd attended since 1988 and all but two of the colleagues I'd worked with since 2005. This is one reason why so many older women with eating disorders and disordered thinking remain uncounted, untreated. Very few people notice. Only my mother and my daughter suggested that I eat more and pick up some weight.

Yet this is not to say that people *didn't* notice. While I was drafting this chapter, I told a woman I had known for twenty-six years that I was writing a memoir about my eating disorders. She said she was relieved. This woman, a member of the Virgo Sisters, a group of three women and me, each with a September birthday, each the recipient of a PhD in English from the University of Nebraska–Lincoln, each the mother of a son and a daughter, each bereaved by the recent loss of a parent at the time we formed our group, a group with whom I had brunch on a regular basis, told me how worried the Sisters had been about my weight loss and the eating behaviors that they had observed at our birthday dinner a couple of years earlier, when, instead of ordering crepes cordon bleu casserole or candied walnut–crusted salmon and wine, as they did, I nibbled at a side salad and sipped water. Yet they didn't feel comfortable saying anything and didn't know what to do. Perhaps other people I knew felt the same. If attention was what I was seeking by becoming smaller and more withered, semistarving wasn't the way to get it. Once again, the causes of eating disorders in older women are deeper, more complex, and more culturally damning than simply wanting to get the attention of the drummers and the trumpet players in the high school band or distressing over the loss of one's waistline or despairing that one doesn't look as good as an air-brushed photograph of an impossibly thin celebrity who, instead of holding down a full-time job and tending to her home and family, spends hours a day at the gym with a pricey personal trainer. Yet not being noticed *does* contribute to my malady.

Eating disorders and disordered eating in older women, which includes those who have suffered from a chronic disorder since adolescence, those, like me, who were long in remission but have relapsed, and the smallest group, those who have manifested symptoms for the first time, differ from those found in girls and young women in several ways. First, we're more likely to restrict than to binge and purge. (I never binge or purge.) Second, in their study of fifty women who developed eating disorders after the age of forty, Edward J. Cumella and Zina Kally, both formerly of the Remuda Ranch Center for Anorexia and Bulimia, discovered that while adolescent female inpatients with eating disorders score high on the Eating Disorder Inventory on "the drive for thinness, bulimia, and body dissatisfaction measures," older female inpatients score higher on the "ineffectiveness, perfectionism, interpersonal distrust, and asceticism scales." Though we care about our jiggly thighs and pouchy bellies, it's not to the same extent that our adolescent counterparts do. Apparently what matters more to us than body image is meeting the unrealistically high standards that we set for ourselves. Third, most experts that I've read see a link between loss, grief, and depression and the onset of an eating disorder in middle-aged and older women. While depression may trigger eating disorders and disordered eating, research suggests that the starvation and malnourishment associated with those conditions can create imbalances in neurotransmitters, chemicals that allow brain cells to communicate and also serve to control appetite and digestion, sleep, mood, thinking, and memory. In short, eating disorders may be caused by depression and may *cause* depression. Anxiety is also prevalent among those with eating disorders. While depression may develop before or during the onset of the disorder, anxiety is more commonly found prior to onset for females of all ages; it was surely a predisposing factor for me when I was fifteen and twenty-five. Fourth, older women are more likely to suffer serious complications from restricting, such as osteoporosis or cardiac problems, than their younger counterparts, in part because their bodies aren't as resilient as those of teenagers and twenty-somethings, but, too, because many have had a longer history with the disease and the associated malnutrition.

While recent research strongly implicates genetic factors as a cause of eating disorders, there's more to the condition than just that. Certainly, a materialistic and patriarchal society that insists that a healthy female body is not only lacking but will never be good enough is at least partly to blame. And, too, if our genes have been there since conception, why would an eating disorder wait fifteen or fifty years to manifest for the first time? In *Gaining: The Truth about Life after Eating Disorders,* Aimee Liu answers that "genetics make the gun, environment loads the gun, and an overwhelming set of emotional circumstances pulls the trigger." And so, when an eating disorder, a disease caused by a combination of genetic and environmental factors, manifests for the first time or returns after many years, we must ask what circumstances *triggered* it. Usually for teenagers and young women, symptoms appear as a result of problems in their family of origin. But middle-aged women are more likely to develop symptoms as a result of changes in their family of choice, the family they created through marriage, cohabitation, procreation, or adoption. Common triggers for older women include separation, divorce, infidelity, or other relationship conflicts; loss of fertility; an empty nest; a child with medical, emotional, or legal problems; the emotional and physical demands of caring for a sick or aged parent or parents; financial strains; and their own health problems. Those female friends and acquaintances of mine who I suspect have eating disorders or periods of disordered eating say that their weight loss was caused by the fear or sadness of an unexpected divorce, cancer (their own or a loved one's), the fear created by a food-borne illness, food allergies, a child in crisis, or scorn from a mate regarding their physical appearance. But none have mentioned aging as the finger that pulled the trigger.

It is no surprise to me that I began restricting again in 2011. For a year or two prior to relapse, I was at times unbearably sad and felt that my life had no purpose. Ian, then twenty-six, had, after several bumpy starts, moved on with his adult life. Meredith, then twenty, was preparing to audition for graduate schools in faraway places. The members of my birth family and some of my dearest friends were far away. In my house, there were four bedrooms, two bathrooms, four chairs at the dining room table, and a two-stall garage, but I used only one of each. Because of the demands of working and single parenting, I hadn't forged enough bonds with people outside of my family while my children were still at home. Dating was a stressful or demoralizing waste of time. Some of the men I kept company with wanted to become exclusive at once, with marriage not far off, which made me feel that just about any woman who said yes would suffice, so it wasn't me as an individual that they were responding to. More of the men I dated wanted me to be a good sport about sharing their time and attention with several other attractive, intelligent middle-aged women. I wasn't particularly interested in getting married, but I certainly wasn't joining a harem.

I was fiercely alone and sad. Hope had evaporated, leaving behind a dry and salty residue. Often, I was fretted by a nagging sense of pointlessness. I'd awaken deep in the night with a ripe ache or with hard knots of grief that made it difficult for me to fall back asleep. Several times I said to myself that I simply could not or would not continue living this way, though I didn't want to think about the alternatives.

The last time I'd felt this ungrounded, or rather, that the bottom had fallen out, was when I was freshly divorced, I was living in a place where I knew few people, and Meredith was spending more of her time at her father's home in Nebraska than mine in Illinois. Though the family I had created and disrupted through divorce was nothing like the Waltons—several generations of a big, well-adjusted family, living and loving under one roof—my house and life had been full and I had known that I was needed and valued. My post-divorce depression was relatively short-lived. I soon made friends. I kept busy with writing, teaching, and mentoring. I often hiked with friends or graduate students in the Shawnee National Forest, a beautiful and magical yet disconcerting place, so unlike my prairie home. I applied for jobs closer to home. Eventually, I accepted an exceptionally good part-time teaching position, quit my job, and moved back to Nebraska so my family could be together again more of the time. But the grief and purposelessness and hungry ache that accompanied the departure of my adult son and daughter weren't so easily fixed. I missed little conversations as one of them passed through the kitchen where I was washing dishes, missed helping them solve their everyday problems or celebrate their everyday successes, missed finding a towel other than my own drying in the bathroom, missed waking up at night and knowing that I wasn't alone in the house. At age fifty-four, I was depressed and anxious, but I didn't want to return to therapy because I already knew what the therapist would tell me: bring more people into your life, become involved with activities that you love and can lose yourself in, get your mind off yourself by helping others, take more risks, love and forgive yourself . . . and consider taking drugs for the depression and anxiety.

My introverted, self-conscious, and perfectionistic hardwiring worked against me in this situation. Rather than risking the self-exposure that came from asserting myself in new and people-y situations, I preferred to stay home and read a good book or take a long, solitary walk at Pioneers Park. I didn't want to take an antidepressant because I believe that, in many cases, rather than prompting one to find and address the cause of one's pain, they merely ease it. And I was wary of the side effects. So I sought to control all that seemed so beyond my control by doing what I'd done before in such situations: I ate very little. Obsessing about food, eating, health, and weight filled my time and gave me purpose. The discomfort of hunger was one that I was in control of and could end anytime I wanted to—or so I told myself. Just as when I was fifteen, I felt that when I denied myself the food that I needed, some fatal flaw was being corrected. Eventually, I'd be rewarded for this, though at the time, I didn't know what that reward might be other than weighing less.

More important than understanding my relapse from an intellectual standpoint is that I came to *feel* the deeper truth about it, through a revelation that I came to in a roundabout way and that showed me why my old friend-foe-ally-adversary had reappeared at this point in my life, leaving me thin and shriveled and thinking too much about food and weight instead of how to change my corner of the world for the better or undertaking relationships and projects that would make my heart sing. Several years earlier, a dear friend had given me a copy of Joyce Tenneson's *Wise Women: A Celebration of Their Insights, Courage, and Beauty*, a stunning collection of tritone photographs of women ages sixty-five to a hundred. I had thanked my friend as I halfheartedly flipped through the pages. I recall being mildly uncomfortable viewing the younger and the younger-looking women, like slender, vivacious sixty-seven-year-old Gloria Steinem in tight leather pants and with long, flowing hair; unlined Tippi Hedren, who, unlike most other women in the book, didn't list her age; taut and slender

Lauren Bacall, looking elegant and defiant at seventy-seven. But when I beheld the older and the older-looking ones, like seventy-year-old Krista Gottlieb, draped in a sheath in such a way that it reveals her missing breast, or gaunt, eighty-five-year-old Mimi Weddell, who, with closed eyes, wispy gray hair, a finely wrinkled face, prominent collarbones, knobby shoulders, and a sheet draped around her just above her nipples, looked as if she were being prepared for a wake, my stomach rolled with revulsion. Oh, how I dread becoming an old woman, I blurted out to God and myself.

After my friend left, I wondered what to do with the book. I couldn't get rid of it because someone I love had given it to me ("June 23, 2003 / To Lisa — In hopes that we, too, will grow into 'wise women.' Thanks for your enduring friendship," my friend had written on the title page). But I didn't have to leave it out where I'd have to see it. I slipped it beneath a stack of *Yoga Journals* in the guest bedroom and more or less forgot about it. Yet, eleven years later, when I was starting to write this book and trying to understand why my malady returned when it did, I remembered the book, pulled it out, and pored over the photographs. On the front cover is sixty-seven-year-old Christine Lee. Her white hair is pulled back, her upper body is nude, and she encloses her lined face with her hands, which form two right angles. Was she pulling up the skin, as I sometimes do when I want to remember what my face looked like before decades of gravity's pull? No. She was putting no pressure on her beautiful, serene face: she was simply framing it.

I studied the women in the photos anew and for the first time read the brief philosophical statements that accompanied the images. When I read Lauren Bacall's comment that she'd like to move out of her Upper West Side apartment building, the Dakota, but couldn't because she'd accumulated too much stuff, I no longer found her unlined face as appealing. When I read cadaverous-looking Mimi Weddell's testimony that unless she reads Shakespeare before going to bed each night, she doesn't feel as alive, I found her incredibly beautiful and someone I'd like to know. When I read sixty-seven-year-old Jane Goodall's statement, "I have used the wisdom I've gained from studying the chimpanzee for forty years and I now travel three hundred days a year in order to share my message with the world. I couldn't have done that when I was younger," and when I read ninety-year-old Phyllis Silverman's statement, "This is a great period in my life. My challenge now is to paint with my true voice. I've been painting all my life, but somehow I still haven't been able to express my deepest vision. Not yet, that is!" I realized that I was reading succinct little resistance narratives, two of many in the book. These narratives challenge the notion that aging in women must involve loss of authority and autonomy. In other words, these women possessed the very things that I felt were waning in my life: power and purpose.

The master narrative that our culture imparts about aging is that midlife and beyond is a time of inexorable decline marked by decay, deterioration, obsolescence, and growing powerlessness, dependency, and irrelevance—a belief that I had long accepted without questioning but now, as an older woman, was having a hard time "swallowing." Our marginalization of the older members of our society and lack of identification with them allow us to harbor a dangerous belief: that they've grown older but we won't. Through such beliefs, and through our condescension or avoidance, we do violence to the aged and to ourselves since, barring an untimely death, we will also become old. To keep our illusions intact, we do violence to the no-longer-young by expecting them to drop out of our view by living and socializing primarily with others their own age or by hiding their age with collagen creams, hair dyes, estrogen supplements, long hours at the gym, weight-reducing diets, and surgeries to lift and tighten loose and lovely fallen flesh. By failing to examine our feelings about aging and gender, by distorting, scorning, or denying our own aging process, we also do violence to ourselves. For some older women, it's the fear of aging that is a trigger, ignition switch, or motivating force for eating disorders. Ironically, by restricting or binging, one intensifies the wrinkles, the wizened features or the sagging, heaviness, the health problems, and the self-absorption that make one appear older than she is. Now I keep *Wise Women* on the coffee table in my living room for my guests and me to look through so we will consider our gerontophobia, our ageism, our fear and loathing of an older woman's body, the culturally induced trauma of aging, and the power of crafting our own life-supportive narratives about old age as a time of power, passion, wisdom, insight, and inner growth. I hope that if I tell myself that resistance story often enough, I'll embrace it and live it.

I've long believed that as a writer whose work is published, read, and honored, as a professor whose students value my knowledge and experience, as the mother of a son and daughter, both of whom have grown up to be charmingly unconventional, and as one who seeks to dwell with God and in God's word, I was immune not to aging but to the stigma of aging, and that I was strong enough to resist the decline-through-aging narrative, a story that is so pervasive and sticky that we can't help but absorb it and pass it on. But I'm not that resilient. I dread entering the country of old age, which—in spite of the cheerful assurances that sixty is the new forty, seventy the new fifty—in my mind begins at sixty (soon, for me). It's infuriating to know that it doesn't have to be this way. By restricting my food intake, I enjoy a sense of power and control at a time when I am told, directly and indirectly, that as an older woman I should be experiencing a loss of power and control. When I go to bed hungry or only eat foods from a narrow and narrowing list of possibilities or spend too many hours a day exercising or lie about having just eaten a gut-splittingly big meal so I don't have to take more than a small plate of fruit from the buffet, it's because I've got a fight on my hands—against my own attitudes and those of my culture about aging. At its core, my restricting is about the desire to rid myself of pain, frustration, and shame. But it's a protest, balm, and purification that cannot inspire me to live a richer, deeper life, and it achieves nothing of real value.

CHAPTER TEN

THE THIRD CHOICE

How does one recover from a malady that is caused and fed by a complex mixture of genetic, biological, and familial factors, as well as various cultural influences, including our culture's idolization of skinny, malnourished women and our disregard for or disdain, even, of aging women? And what, exactly, is recovery? According to the dictionary, to "recover" means "to return to a normal state of health, mind or strength; to find or regain possession of something lost or stolen." What I have lost, or perhaps what has been stolen from me because of my malady, is a right and natural response to my physiological sensations: eating when hungry; not eating when not hungry. What I have lost, or perhaps what has been stolen from me, are the innocence, honesty, trust, and freedom that once surrounded that fundamental act of nourishing the body, mind, and soul. What I have lost, or perhaps what has been stolen from me, are all the time and energy that I invested in such a fruitless endeavor as weighing as little as possible. Can any of this be restored or returned to me?

Some experts define recovery from an eating disorder or disordered eating as the return to and maintenance of normal weight or body mass. Yet one can have a normal body size but still have an intense fear of gaining weight or a disturbance in how one sees her body. Other experts define recovery as the abatement or moderation of obvious symptoms, such as weighing oneself a dozen times a day or purging or refusing to eat more than a thimbleful of soup for dinner, as well as those symptoms that are harder to see and treat, such as a low self-esteem that doesn't match one's accomplishments, social fears, and unrealistically high expectations of oneself—deeply embedded traits that I've been chipping away at with the help of various therapists for the past three decades. Abatement is not a release from symptoms; rather, it is a diminishment in their frequency and severity. When I consider the level of restricting and anxiety I endured during the several months that led up to and followed that road trip across Nebraska, Missouri, Illinois, and Indiana during the summer of 2011, I can say that my symptoms have diminished. For that, I'm grateful. But they are not gone. While my weight is holding steady and I feel and look healthier than I did in 2011 and 2012, I still tally calories every day on little slips of paper that I carry in my pocket or wallet or leave on the kitchen counter. This is a pointless activity since I eat more or less the same amount of the same things every day. I still feel panic if my weight slides up a few pounds. I still sometimes lie about what I've eaten and occasionally about how much I weigh (when I last renewed my driver's license, I rounded up to the next nearest ten). I still feel I'm unworthy of fullness and abundance, and still fear how fat, unruly, and repulsive I might become without my old friend and foe to keep me in line. Even now, I still feel the perplexing lure of not eating as a way of getting even with someone who has done me wrong or as a way to punish myself.

Some experts say that one has recovered from an eating disorder or disordered eating when relapse is no longer a threat. For instance, Kathleen M. Pike, a professor of psychology at Columbia University Medical Center, defines recovery as the point at which an individual who has previously been diagnosed with anorexia nervosa is symptom-free and at a comparable risk for the manifestation of symptoms as a matched control in the general population. The first criterion is clear, but the second is not. What is normal if, as clinical psychologist Stacey M. Rosenfeld points out in *Does Every Woman Have an Eating Disorder?*, "almost every woman has an eating disorder of sorts—not necessarily anorexia, bulimia, or binge eating per se, but a fixation on food, weight, and shape that is unhealthy, unwanted, and undying"? Is this the "normal" against which a woman should compare herself?

Several studies in recent years have asked people with anorexia what they think recovery means. Almost all say that for them, recovery consists of restoring physical health and overcoming the "anorexic mind-set." The responses that most resonate with me, and, I suspect, with other people with eating disorders and disordered eating, are those recorded and classified by Mary M. H. Lamoureux and Joan L. Bottorff in "'Becoming the Real Me': Recovering from Anorexia Nervosa" in 2005. The study authors interviewed nine women who had recovered from anorexia, ranging in age from nineteen to forty-eight, eight of whom were of the restricting subtype and one of whom was of the binging and purging subtype. Based on what the women said about their experiences, the researchers were able to break down the process of recovery into five psychological categories. First, recovery means that one is able to recognize the dangers of the disease, something that is obscured by the fear of gaining weight when one is deep into the illness. Second, recovery isn't a dramatic leap from sickness to health but an "inching out of anorexia" that involves both "tiny, tiny baby steps" and a "forward and backward" movement. Third, recovery means "tolerating exposure without anorexia," which entails those with anorexia letting go of the defenses and security that the condition provides and revealing "their true feelings of insecurity, powerlessness, and not knowing who they [are]." Fourth, recovery means "becoming aware of and deconstructing distorted ideas about [the act of] eating making them 'bad' persons, about not deserving food, and about how being smaller mean[s] making smaller mistakes," as well as "challeng[ing] their strongly held beliefs and misperceptions that anorexia [is] the only means of achieving a sense of control, identity, and self-worth." Fifth, recovery means "discovering and reclaiming self as 'good enough'" and seeing oneself as valuable and worthy in spite of how much one weighs. What most closely matches my experience of my malady is the idea that while a change in one's mind-set might happen by great leaps of faith and intention, more likely is the "inching out of" movement that the women in the study refer to: creeping forward and falling backward, creeping and falling, with success best measured by the scant teaspoonful. And, too, I find the image of recovery as a stripping away or shedding of layers of defenses and cognitive distortions until one reaches the pure and healthy self that is still there in spite of decades of illness both true and inspiring.

Lamoureux and Bottorff observe that those with anorexia and those with other mental illnesses agree that recovery is a process of "rediscovering one's sense of self" or "becoming the real me." Yet there's a critical difference between the two groups. Recovery for those with schizophrenia, major depression, and anxiety disorder means "acknowledging the mental illness as a part of one's self-identity." In contrast, the women in Lamoureux and Bottorff's study didn't consider themselves recovered until "they no longer identified anorexia as a part of who they were." I suspect that for most with eating disorders or who are on the anorectic side of the disordered-eating spectrum, it's easier to quit restricting than it is to relinquish the identity that the condition provides.

Part of my identification with my malady is that I'm so drawn to the metaphors, the contradictions, and the striking tensions associated with it: restricting as problem and solution, as refuge and prison; restricting as an attempt to fill the emptiness with hunger, denial, or disappearance or extinction of the self; restricting as a way of both conquering and succumbing to one's appetites; restricting as a way to take charge by shrinking one's hips and breasts, stopping ovulation, and returning to that prepubescent, nonsexualized time in life before one had to choose between being a self-confident woman who claims her right to take up space and being a voiceless, obedient woman who lives small; restricting as the symptom of a controlling and potentially health-compromising condition that one must be secretive about since the uninformed view it as a character flaw or moral failing; and restricting as the symptom of an illness that one revels in since people admire and envy the afflicted's thinness and self-control. Who, asks the woman or girl who restricts, would she be if she gave up these tantalizing paradoxes?

While the experts not only disagree about what constitutes recovery from an eating disorder or disordered eating, most of what they say about it concerns only adolescents and young women. Yet the age of the one with the disorder affects the definition of and method of recovery. In *The Oxford Handbook of Child and Adolescent Eating Disorders,* James Lock, a professor of psychiatry and behavioral medicine at Stanford University School of Medicine, says that it's reasonable to have different expectations and standards for remission and recovery in younger patients, who may be more responsive to treatment, than in those who have been "chronically disordered" for decades. Certainly the therapeutic issues are different for a woman in her fifties who in spite of her successes and sacrifices is seen by herself and others as being old and beside the point than for her adolescent counterpart who is primarily responding to conflicts within her birth family. In a study published in the *Journal of Psychological Science* in 2011, Australian researchers Sian L. Mclean, Susan J. Paxton, and Eleanor H. Wertheim found that a group of sixty-one women with disordered eating ages thirty to sixty who participated in just eight weeks of cognitive behavioral therapy focused on "midlife themes" were still doing better in terms of "body image, disordered eating, and risk factors" at the follow-up six months later than a control group that had not had that opportunity.

I am hopeful about my reclamation of my once-healthier relationship with hunger, food, and body. One reason for this is that my life is richer and more satisfying than it was at the time of the most recent onset of my malady, in 2011. When my children were living at home, I was so busy tending to them, trying to earn enough money to cover the bills, and, in whatever time I had left, writing essays and books that I had no need for anyone or anything else. I had a robust appetite and ate until I was full, giving little thought to food, eating, or my weight. But then the long, full, satisfied period ended. At the time of the most recent onset of my malady, the departure of my son and my daughter left me feeling sad and unable to imagine anything that would fill the void created by their gutting absence.

I found the remedy for my malady in what I call the "replacement theory," which I developed after I read the chapter titled "Hunger" in Naomi Wolf's book *The Beauty Myth: How Images of Beauty Are Used against Women*. Actually, that's not entirely true. I discovered the remedy during the Gray Years, when I realized that by feeding my hungers for God, art, and social action, and by creating a ceremony involving bread, I could experience fullness. But somehow I'd forgotten about this antidote until I read Wolf's "Hunger."

Wolf connects the explosion and exponential growth of eating disorders in the sixties, seventies, and beyond to a backlash against the gains made by Western women during that time period—gains such as the opening of formerly male-only professions and institutions of higher education to women; legal protections against discrimination; the legalization of birth control and abortion, which made possible sexual freedom and freedom from unwanted motherhood; and the possibility of economic independence. But there was stiff and widespread resistance to these gains. "When women came en masse into male spheres," Wolf argues, "that pleasure [of 'women's natural fullness'] had to be overridden by an urgent social expedient that would make women's bodies into the prisons that their homes no longer were." All one had to do to quiet a woman with high aspirations was convince her that she was overweight, even though she wasn't, and that her "ideal" weight was one stone, or fourteen pounds, below her natural, healthy weight, thus redefining her natural shape and size as too big. Thereafter, says Wolf, "a wave of self-hatred swept over First World women, a reactionary psychology was perfected, and a major industry [weight loss] was born." The anorectic may have begun her journey bold and defiant, but from the perspective of a male-centered society, she ended up as the "perfect woman . . . weak, sexless, and voiceless" and very, very obedient. I can attest that a woman whose focus has narrowed to the twelve celery sticks and the tablespoon of fat-free ranch dressing on her plate and the number on the scale is not a woman with the time or mental and physical energy to claim her power, speak her mind, live large, or love fully.

Even though I take issue with Wolf's simplistic view that eating disorders are caused by just one factor, the reaction of a patriarchal culture to women's growing freedoms, instead of the tangle of physical, mental, and sociocultural factors that I see, I am nonetheless strengthened and empowered by her thinking. No, it's a rawer feeling than that. I feel fighting mad when I read Wolf's statement that during her anorexic year, "all the space I had for dreaming was taken up by food." How does one recover a lost year? she asks. "Who is obliged to make reparations to me for the thought abandoned, the energy never found, the explorations never considered? Who owes me for the year-long occupation of a mind at the time of its most urgent growth?" With this, Wolf has given me something clear and defined to push against. I won't let my malady take anything else from me.

According to the replacement theory, every minute in which I'm overexercising or obsessing about food, calories, proportions, weight, and my failures and inadequacies, I'm not putting my precious time and energy toward something that will bear good fruit. Like what? I ask myself. This is a harder question than it seems because it requires some dreaming and indulgence. It involves believing that one deserves something good—and those of us with eating disorders and disordered eating are quite convinced of our unworthiness. But if I push through this resistance, I can admit that I'd like to use the time and energy that I spend overexercising and thinking about food to become fluent in another language; to learn to dance—salsa, line, buck, jazz, jitterbug; to learn to grow, prepare, and prescribe herbs to help others heal; to expand my circle of friends and to be in closer touch with old friends, both those who are near and those who are far away; and to use my communication skills and faith in shalom, the biblical model of peace, wholeness, and justice, to make more visible the faces and forces that create and allow poverty to exist in this wealthiest of nations. To fill our heart's desires, women must, as Wolf says, "liberate the occupied territories of our minds and energies." When one's homeland is occupied, one has options: one can submit, leave, go into hiding, or take on the tyrant who captured or seized what was once free or one's own with everything one's got.

When I found myself grief-stricken in 2011, I pushed hard against the obvious: I had to create and embrace a new identity that no longer was primarily defined by my relationships with my son and daughter and forge connections with people who could "replace" the companionship I once had with my children. Bringing people into my life required more strength and tenacity than I had expected. For one thing, it meant going against my hardwiring and forcing the quiet, self-conscious introvert in me, who would rather stay home and write or putter around the house or yard, to leave my refuge and socialize with people. Also, it meant seeking people who were willing to be my friends. I discovered that gregarious folks already had connections in place, and the less social ones tended not to want them. I extended invitations to my acquaintances and prayed that they would become my friends. Initially, most people accepted my invitations but seldom or never returned them. Even though many people my age were busy with jobs and family (some still had children at home; those with grandchildren placed high priority on babysitting and attending dance recitals and ballgames), and like most of us in this time and place, they were frittering away too much of their leisure time by staring at time-devouring electronic screens, I took each refusal personally. When some didn't accept my invitations or accepted but didn't reciprocate, I crossed them off my list. But with those who seemed more promising, I kept forgiving, kept asking, kept trying not to dwell on the lack of reciprocation. While it took a couple of years of prayer and persistence, I was finally blessed with several friends who are as enthusiastic about my company as I am about theirs. I have two friends with whom I have a standing date each week—one for lunch, one for a long walk on a bike and pedestrian trail. I have several other friends that I see on a less structured basis. Every once in a while, I'll muster up my resolve and date a bit—more because I feel I should than because I want or need a man in my life.

I returned to the tiny church that I'd been a member of since 1988 but had drifted away from when Ian was in trouble and I needed stronger spiritual guidance and support. While on Saturday evenings I go to a large church where I hear life-changing sermons and take Communion, eating, with no reservations, the gluten-free wafer that I dip in wine, I've come to realize that my old, staid Sunday morning church offers something that I need just as much—a robust community and the continuity of being with people who remember me as a graduate student, as a married woman and mother, and now as a professional woman who lives alone, carries a raggedy, worn-out, marked-up Bible, and serves on church committees only with great coaxing and flattery. They remember my son and daughter as children in Sunday school or Bible school or Christmas pageants. Likewise, I remember them and their children and grandchildren at different stages of their lives. Now I'm there most Sunday mornings for the service and the fellowship that follows. Through the Heartland Big Brothers Big Sisters Program, I became a mentor and buddy to a preteen girl, with whom I play flute duets, bake cookies, and go to movies, plays, farmer's markets, and the nature center, and to whom I give what I hope is sound advice about attracting or deflecting attention from guys, about managing all those rules at school and each of her parents' homes, and about whether she should become a veterinarian, a stay-at-home mom, a country western singer, or a cop. I am part of a team of volunteers that prepares and serves meals to the homeless and near homeless at an outreach center. My students continue to provide affirmation, and through my teaching and mentoring, I'm creating a legacy. If my third episode of disordered eating and thinking was triggered by a depression rooted in an empty house, a lonesome life, and fear that as an aging woman, others saw me as insignificant, then I can keep myself safe from relapse by nourishing relationships with people who not only *see* me but find me relevant and valuable.

During the Grieving Season, I was struck by the realization that I no longer wanted to write about nature, the environment, and regionalism. Even more, the thought of writing another nature essay about Nebraska or the Great Plains literally nauseated me. I was puzzled by this strong, visceral response. Being a nature writer was, after all, a vital part of my identity. But after twenty-six years of writing and publishing nature essays, I'd lost my appetite for my subject. In part I was finished with this subject because I'd said everything I had to say about nature. There were no diminished habitats that I wanted to eulogize, no despoilers of nature that I wanted to expose and rebuke, no arguments that I wanted to advance about biocentrism over anthropocentrism, about native versus introduced species, no further explorations about nature as a social construct or the dangers of turning organisms or natural processes into metaphors that I wanted to undertake, no wild or wildish places that I wanted to celebrate. Been there, done that. But, too, nature writing, as I practiced it, was a largely solitary endeavor. Now I'm far more interested in pursuing subjects that connect me to other people and their creations or that explore my relationship with others (individuals, communities, God). Because I seldom experienced that human connection, which I always craved, when writing about the natural world, I had to stop thinking of myself as "just" a nature writer and open myself up to other subjects. Now I suspect that I wrote about nature to avoid writing directly about myself. But through the expansion of my subject matter that led to the writing of this book, I've lessened the distance between myself and my subject.

Writing this book is also part of the healing. But it's been difficult. This project has demanded that I reenter those dark times when I lived deep within the "occupied territory" and hadn't the strength, will, or desire to face the occupying force. It was difficult to expose thoughts and behaviors I preferred to keep hidden. It was difficult to limit the things I wrote about other people that they might find uncomfortable or hurtful but that seemed essential to the story, or to remain silent and so compromise my reflections and analysis. It was difficult to read the research on eating disorders and disordered eating and accept that to some extent, this affliction is due to my genetic heritage, which I cannot change, as well as to some pretty potent and intractable cultural forces, which I can try to resist. And then there's this: by going public with my story, I have a greater responsibility to become and stay well—whether I want that every minute of every day or not. Indeed, because of these factors, I deliberated about whether I really wanted to write, much less publish, the story of my malady.

Writing my memoir was literally sickening and injurious. When I was drafting the last few chapters of this book, I had several ailments, including such bad tendonitis in both forearms that it hurt to slice a carrot, much less strike letters on a keyboard; a knee injury that resulted in an egglike mass at the back of my right knee that left me sore and gimpy for a few weeks; a yeast infection (my first in many, many years); two rounds of wasp stings (the second round caused my left hand and arm to swell to painful, hideous proportions); stomach flu (I vomited for the first time this century); and worst of all, a three-week case of shingles, the first week and a half of which was scream-out-loud excruciating. "What's going on with your head?" my Wednesday morning walk buddy asked me when I got her up to date on my most recent ailment. I told her that I believed it was connected with the writing of my memoir. "You're releasing obstructions, cleaning house," she said. "It may be hard now but ultimately, it's good." I agreed.

Another reason that writing this book has been so challenging is that I don't know if I'm seeing myself and my malady clearly. After all, denial of the seriousness of one's illness is one of the diagnostic features of some eating disorders and disordered eating. In "Dealing with Denial in Anorexia Nervosa," Walter Vandereycken says that what those with anorexia deny are the physical features of the disorder as well as those behaviors they use to cope with their "social surroundings" and to hide their disease. Vandereycken says that research on the denial of those with anorexia has been "hampered by a lack of agreement as to whether it is conscious or unconscious, a trait versus a state, an indication of psychological disturbance, or a functional coping mechanism." If denial is part of the disease, how can one trust a person with anorexia or disordered eating to be straight with the facts and to tell a complete and honest story about herself? I had truly believed for a few years that to be healthy, I had to drastically change my diet in response to GERD and gluten sensitivity. I now believe instead that because I didn't have the willpower to only eat in moderation the breads and desserts that I love, I made myself sick so I would never again eat these temptations. I also believe that I unconsciously used a misdiagnosed illness and a food sensitivity that is more of a nuisance than a threat to disguise my malady from myself and others. Equally unsettling is that after I became conscious of my motives, I continued with many of the same food-restricting behaviors. Does it matter whether the one with the eating disorder or disordered eating is conscious or unconscious of what she's doing, whether her condition is a psychological disturbance or a defense mechanism, or whether she is consistently, intentionally deceptive (a trait) or her dishonesty is intermittent (a state), if the end result, self-deception, is the same? Once I realized the extent to which I had duped myself, I wondered if I could ever trust myself to know what my true motives are—not just about what and why I am or am not eating but about anything.

Even so, I do have moments of clarity and insight that give me hope. After I began losing weight again in 2011, each lowest weight became my new set point, my new normal. "Never again can I weigh more than this," I'd tell myself as I became lighter and watched the numbers on the scale become more filled with ones and zeros and then only two numbers. A few years later, when I became ill with stomach flu, my weight dropped to a number on the scale that I had last seen in the summer between sixth and seventh grade. I was thrilled and frightened. Then I heard a voice, perhaps mine, perhaps God's, say to me, "This is dangerous. This will not be the new normal." After the flu passed and I started eating again, I watched the number on the scale climb to what it had been before my illness. It was anxiety provoking to let go of that low number. But I had to since I knew how easy it would be to start severely restricting again. I could not let that happen again. For one thing, I haven't the fat reserves to sustain me during another period of prolonged restricting. For another, I don't want all the space I have for dreaming taken up with even more obsessive thoughts about food, weight, and exercise. I count this as a triumph and as evidence of healing. And that is why I lied about my weight when I renewed my driver's license a few days after I'd had the flu. I *would* be gaining that weight back.

As a precaution, I confided in a few people that I'm just one trauma away from relapse, and a trauma at this point in life would most likely involve a deep loss—an inevitable part of aging. While those few people know how to recognize signs that I'm vulnerable and markedly limiting my food intake again, what I perhaps haven't made clear is how cagey and deceptive I can be when I'm restricting. Don't believe me if I tell you that I'm eating more than vegetables and rice cakes, that nothing is wrong, that my weight is stable, that I really do believe that I have a right to take up space and to speak until I'm heard. Believe, instead, what you see.

I continue to be conflicted about my own recovery. While I want to be free of my malady, I also am afraid to live without it since it is such an essential and defining part of my identity. I relish being small and shopping for clothes in the girls' department. This is the size I was meant to be! I tell myself. This is good! Yet when I hear my little sister tell her mother, "Lisa only eats vegetables," I'm embarrassed. Just what am I modeling for this girl? There are dangers within this refuge that I've created for myself.

When Jesus saw an invalid of thirty-eight years waiting to be healed by the Pool of Bethesda, he asked the question that cuts to the heart of the matter: "Do you want to be made well?" The invalid didn't answer. Apparently, he couldn't see or imagine that healing might come to him in a different form than he'd always believed it would. I suspect that most with eating disorders and disordered eating, when asked, "Do you want to be made well?" would either insist that there was nothing wrong with them or firmly reject the invitation. No, we don't want to be made well because that would mean eating more, weighing more, feeling more. No, we don't want to be made well because our disordered-eating thoughts and behaviors give us our sense of self, self-worth, and purpose. By restricting, we can try to defy the forces that intend to weaken or destroy us. Cynthia Bulik likens the attitude of those with eating disorders toward their own recovery to the experience of driving a car with one foot on the accelerator and one on the brake. "One half is ready to embark on the journey, but the other is not ready to relinquish control." And so, rather than being still, centered, harmonious, and at peace, one shakes, rumbles, and burns a lot of fuel while going nowhere.

Because I remember so well the sense of power, exhilaration, and triumph that accompanies becoming smaller, I know how easy it would be for me to court the click and the shift and then watch my weight drop to a number on the scale that I haven't seen since elementary school. When I'm losing weight, I feel clean and pure and powerful. Something wrong or shameful is being righted or validated. Some great reward is at hand. And, too, there is the pleasure of feeling morally superior to those who are stuffing themselves on supersized portions at the restaurant or multiple servings at the buffet line and will feel bloated and guilty afterward. I don't want to get bigger and be part of a society where, according to the Centers for Disease Control and Prevention, over 69 percent of the adults—that's two out of every three adults—are overweight and 35 percent are obese. If that is regular old white bread, I'd rather be dry, bony, and hungry. Yet, those with chafing thighs and those whose thighs never touch are both obsessed with food; both are very, very hungry. There's no difference.

My healing also depends on truthfully answering that most basic question: what am I hungry for that food cannot fill? The old answers pour out. Love. Approval. A sense of belonging. Autonomy. And now I also name this newly realized one: to age in such a way that I feel vital and valuable to myself and others, in spite of the growing invisibility that accompanies female aging in this time and place. But I'm surprised when I also answer that I'm hungry for bread—not just the metaphorical kind, but slices of real bread, made by my own hands in my own kitchen. We cannot live by bread alone; yet our daily bread we must have.

I've long suspected that the answer to my malady would be homeopathic, part of that medical system that seeks to ease or cure disease with remedies that create symptoms similar to those the patient is manifesting. In other words, "like cures like." Minute, homeopathically prepared doses of coffee cure sleeplessness. Minute, homeopathically prepared doses of ipecac syrup cure vomiting. Conventional, allopathic medicine also treats some conditions through the homeopathic principle of the law of similars. Thus, the stimulant Ritalin counters the restlessness and inattention of attention-deficit/hyperactivity disorder; injections of pollen or pet dander desensitize one who is reactive to those allergens. Perhaps by extension, one can heal an eating disorder by taking into one's body the physical and symbolic substance that triggers the binge or becomes the temptation during the fast.

For most of my adult life, I've limited my choices to two: binging on bread; abstaining from bread. The third choice, eating bread in moderation, is one with which I have had little experience. It's a choice that terrifies me. If I bring bread into my home, I might eat, mindlessly eat, and once again, I'm big and disgusted or back to restricting. The third choice is a walk along the narrow way that passes between the dichotomies of mind and body, spirit and flesh, reason and desire, public and private, culture and nature, bread as symbol and bread as physical reality. Christian theologian Marcus Borg refers to the narrow way as "the path of centering in the sacred." Perhaps by creating a ritual that involves making and eating bread that is at once physical and spiritual food, I will be nourished, filled, and healed.

On a Saturday morning almost forty-two years after the first episode of my malady, I close the blinds so I won't be distracted by the cardinals in the forsythia bushes. I light a candle on the dining room table, place a slice of homemade bread on a china dessert plate, pour a glass of water, and sit down. I'm taking this bread straight—no cream cheese, no peanut butter, no jelly, no hummus. When I eat meals alone, which now is most of the time, I often skim the newspaper, scroll through Facebook posts, or listen to NPR. What results is fast, distracted eating—raw consumption. What I am doing here for the next ten minutes is the opposite of that: eating with full and unflinching attention.

I center myself by feeling my feet on the floor, my buttocks on the seat of the chair, and the small of my back firmly against the back of the chair. I soften my breathing, my gaze, and the muscles in my face. I feel my hunger in my stomach, my mouth, and my brain. I offer thanksgiving for this bread, ask for presence of mind, God's protection, and the ability to see this ritual through to the end one more time. This bread will satisfy some of my hungers. But others are beyond the power of any physical food. I must remain clear as to which hungers I'm humbly attending to and which are being left wanting, so I never again hide, forget, deny, or disguise them.

In my mind's eye, I see myself: a small, thin woman, with blue-green eyes, blond hair (though my face is framed by short, wiry gray hairs), a face that is longer than it used to be and etched with both laugh and frown lines, a body still supple from more than thirty years of yoga. I see the dense, brown slice of bread that I will soon take into myself, one slow, deliberate, savoring bite at a time. This is not an ordinary meal but a homeopathic remedy, a strength-building regimen, a spiritual discipline, a sacred rite.

I watch myself take a bite of bread, too small to be a mouthful, and put the slice back on the plate. After I chew and swallow, I pause. Before the next bite, I again center myself. Feet. Buttocks. Small of the back. Breath. Gaze. Hungers. How many calories will I be consuming at this simple meal? About eighty. I'm remarkably accurate when estimating the number of calories in a serving of food, but now I'm anxious and my stomach is full of needles. How careless of me not to have tallied the total number of calories in the entire loaf, measured the length of the loaf and the thickness of the slice on my plate, and then divided the width of this slice into the whole so I'd know the exact number of calories it contains. Seventy-eight? Eighty-two? There's a difference, you know. I start to run the numbers in my head (one-third of a cup of olive oil: 630 calories; two packets of dry yeast: 42 calories . . .). Stop! I don't want to waste this slice of my fleeting life thinking about what cannot fill me or allowing something to keep me from pursuing what can. Feet. Buttocks. Small of the back. Breath. Gaze. Hungers. This slice of bread.

My healing rite involves just one slice of bread and ten minutes of my life spent in the here and now halfway between breakfast and lunch each day. But I don't look forward to it. Many days, I stall. Then I'm both the rule breaker and the rule enforcer. Just let me grade three more essays or answer five more email messages or run a little errand or make a phone call or sort the recycling, I tell myself. Or, since I'm running late for my office hours, would it be okay if I ate the slice in four swift bites while standing at the sink? But I remain firm. What I hope is that my daily bread-eating exercise will eventually release me from my rigid, restrictive thinking. What I'm certain of is that my daily rite keeps me honest and dependent on God.

I watch myself take another small bite of bread and chew slowly, tasting the blend of garbanzo bean, fava bean, sorghum, potato, and tapioca flours; the vinegar, oil, and milk; the yeast that leavens it; and the gums that hold it all together. The texture is grittier and drier than bread made from wheat flour, and it's not as sweet as I like since I forgot to add honey. But it's not perfection I crave but substantial, earthy bread. I let the bread dissolve on my tongue just as I do at Holy Communion, so I can savor the sacrifice and the fulfillment. I swallow and feel the bread moving down my throat. I take a sip of water. Bread and water: prison food. Bread and water: the food of liberation. I pick up the slice, take another small bite, and put it back on the plate.

It's a razor's edge I walk. How tempting it is to wolf down this slice and the rest of the loaf. How tempting it is to throw it into the sink as if it's on fire, douse it with water, and then cram it down the garbage dispos-al. Instead, I remain at my dining room table, eating, poised between the past and the future, between stuff or starve, between what I'm told about myself and what I know to be true, simply eating this slice of bread and attending to the sensations. This act of eating bread with the entirety of my being feels decadent and indulgent. How many of these simple, mindful meals will it take to erase the vestiges of all those times when I denied my desire for bread or ate bread as filler? How many of these simple, mindful meals will it take to provide the fullness I crave? When I've eaten the last crumb, blown out the candle, opened the blind, and set my plate and glass in the sink, I feel relieved that the ritual is done for another day. And yet, the bread was good, and for a moment here and there, I found pleasure in eating it.

SOURCES

American Psychiatric Association. *Diagnostic and Statistical Manual of Mental Disorders.* 5th ed. Arlington, VA: American Psychiatric Publishing, 2013.
———. "Feeding and Eating Disorders." Fact Sheet. DSM5.org. American Psychiatric Publishing. 2013. http://www.dsm5.org/documents/eating %20disorders%20fact%20sheet.pdf.

Arnold, Carrie. *Decoding Anorexia: How Breakthroughs in Science Offer Hope for Eating Disorders.* New York: Routledge, 2012.

Bailer, Ursula F., and Walter H. Kaye. "Serotonin: Imaging Findings in Eating Disorders." In *Behavioral Neurobiology of Eating Disorders,* ed. W. H. Kaye and R. Adan, 59–79. Current Topics in Behavioral Neurosciences 6. Springer-Verlag Berlin Heidelberg, 2011. doi: 10.1007/978-3-642-15131-6.

Beers, Mark H., and Robert S. Potter. *The Merck Manual of Diagnosis and Therapy.* 18th ed. Whitehouse Station, NJ: Merck, 2006.

Bell, Rudolph M. *Holy Anorexia.* Chicago: University of Chicago Press, 1987.

Berrettini, Wade. "Genetic Aspects of Anorexia Nervosa and Bulimia Nervosa." *Directions Psychiatric* 17 (1998): 53–57.

Blakeslee, Sandra. "A Small Part of the Brain, and Its Profound Effects." *New York Times,* February 6, 2007. http://www.nytimes.com/2007/02/06/health /psychology/06brain.html?pagewanted=all&_r=1.

Bordo, Susan. *Unbearable Weight: Feminism, Western Culture, and the Body.* Berkeley: University of California Press, 1993.

Borg, Marcus J. "Narrow Is the Way." Marcus J. Borg Foundation, June 10, 2015. http://www.marcusjborg.com/2010/06/15/narrow-is-the-way/.

Boskind-White, Marlene, and William C. White Jr. *Bulimarexia: The Binge/Purge Cycle and Self-Starvation.* New York: Norton, 1983.

Bratman, Steven, and David Knight. *Health Food Junkies: Orthorexia Nervosa: Overcoming the Obsession with Healthful Eating.* New York: Broadway, 2001.

Bruch, Hilde. *Conversations with Anorexics: A Compassionate and Hopeful Journey through the Therapeutic Process.* New York: Basic Books, 1988.

———. *Eating Disorders: Obesity, Anorexia Nervosa, and the Person Within.* New York: Basic Books, 1973.

———. *The Golden Cage: The Enigma of Anorexia Nervosa.* Cambridge: Harvard University Press, 1978.

———. "Psychotherapy in Primary Anorexia Nervosa." *Journal of Nervous and Mental Disease* 150, no. 1 (1970): 51–66.

Bulik, Cynthia M. *Midlife Eating Disorders: Your Journey to Recovery.* New York: Walker, 2013.

Bulik, Cynthia M., Federica Tozzi, Charles Anderson, Suzanne Mazzeo, Steve Aggen, and Patrick F. Sullivan. "The Relation between Eating Disorders and Components of Perfectionism." *American Journal of Psychiatry* 160, no. 2 (2003): 366–68.

Bynum, Caroline Walker. *Holy Feast, Holy Fast: The Religious Significance of Food to Medieval Women.* Oakland: University of California Press, 1988.

Catherine of Siena. *Saint Catherine of Siena as Seen in Her Letters.* Trans. Vida D. Scudder. London: 1905.

Chernin, Kim. *Obsessions: Reflections on the Tyranny of Slenderness.* New York: Harper & Row, 1981.

Couser, G. Thomas. *Recovering Bodies: Illness, Disability, and Life Writing.* Madison: University of Wisconsin Press, 1997.

Cumella, Edward J., and Zina Kally. "Profile of 50 Women with Midlife-Onset Eating Disorders." *Eating Disorders: The Journal of Treatment & Prevention* 16, no. 3 (2008): 193–203.

Dass, Ram. *Be Here Now.* San Cristobel, NM: Lama Foundation, 1971.

Demaret, Kent. "Psychiatrist Hilde Bruch Saves Anorexia Nervosa Patients from Starving Themselves to Death." *People,* June 26, 1978. http://www.people.com/people/archive/article/0,,20071146,00.html.

Dillard, Annie. *The Best American Essays 1988.* Boston: Houghton Mifflin, 1988.

Findlay, Sheri. "Dieting in Adolescence." *Paediatrics & Child Health* 9, no. 7 (2004): 487–91.

Frost, Christopher J., and Rebecca Bell-Metereau. *Simone Weil: On Politics, Religion, and Society.* Los Angeles: SAGE, 1998.

Gagne, Danielle A., Ann Von Halle, Kimberly A. Brownley, Cristin D. Runfola, Sara Hofmeier, Kateland E. Branch, and Cynthia M. Bulik. "Eating Disorder

Symptoms and Weight and Shape Concerns in a Large Web-Based Convenience Sample of Women Ages 50 and Above: Results of the Gender and Body Image (GABI) Study." *International Journal of Eating Disorders* 45, no. 7 (2012): 832–44.

Goeree, Michelle Sovinsky, John C. Ham, and Daniela Iorio. "Race, Social Class, and Bulimia Nervosa." IZA Discussion Paper No. 5823. July 4, 2011. Available at SSRN: http://ssrn.com/abstract=1877636.

Grice, D. E., K. A. Halmi, M. M. Fichter, M. M. Strober, D. B. Woodside, J. T. Treasure, A. S. Kaplan, P. J. Magistretti, D. Goldman, C. M. Bulik, and W. H. Berrettini. "Evidence for a Susceptibility Gene for Anorexia Nervosa on Chromosome." *American Journal of Human Genetics* 70, no. 3 (2002): 787–92.

Halmi, K. A., S. R. Sunday, M. Strober, A. Kaplan, D. B. Woodside, M. Fichter, J. Treasure, W. H. Berrettini, and W. Kaye. "Perfectionism in Anorexia Nervosa: Variation by Clinical Subtype, Obsessionality, and Pathological Eating Behavior." *American Journal of Psychiatry* 157, no. 11 (2000): 1799–1805.

Helwig, Maggie. "Hunger." In *Best Canadian Essays 1990,* ed. Douglas Fetherling. Markham, ON: Fifth House, 1990.

Hoerburger, Rob. "Karen Carpenter's Second Life." *New York Times Magazine,* October 6, 1996. http://www.nytimes.com/1996/10/06/magazine /karen-carpenter-s-second-life.html?pagewanted=all.

Hudson, James I., E. Hiripi, H. G. Pope, and R. C. Kessler. "The Prevalence and Correlates of Eating Disorders in the National Comorbidity Survey Replication." *Biological Psychiatry* 61, no. 3 (2007): 348–58.

Irwin, Alec. "Devoured by God: Cannibalism, Mysticism, and Ethics in Simone Weil." *Cross Currents* 51, no. 2 (Summer 2001).

Kaye, Walter H., Ursula F. Bailer, Megan Klabunde, and Harriet Brown. "Is Anorexia Nervosa an Eating Disorder? How Neurobiology Can Help Us Understand the Puzzling Eating Symptoms of Anorexia Nervosa." Eating Disorders Center for Treatment and Research, University of California, San Diego. http://eatingdisorders.ucsd.edu/research/biocorrelates/PDFs/Kay-e2010NeurobiologyofAN.pdf.

Kaye, Walter H., Cynthia M. Bulik, L. Thornton, N. Barbarich, and K. Masters. "Comorbidity of Anxiety Disorders with Anorexia and Bulimia Nervosa." *American Journal of Psychiatry* 161, no. 12 (2004): 2215–21.

Kaye, Walter H., and T. E. Weltzin. "Serotonin Activity in Anorexia and Bulimia Nervosa: Relationship to the Modulation of Feeding and Mood." *Journal of Clinical Psychiatry* 52 (1991): 41–48.

Klump, K. L., P. K. Keel, C. Sisk, and S. A. Burt. "Preliminary Evidence That Estradiol Moderates Genetic Influences on Disordered Eating Attitudes and Behaviors during Puberty." *Psychological Medicine* 40, no. 10 (2010): 1745–53.

Klump, Kelly L. "Puberty as a Critical Risk Period for Eating Disorders: A Review of Human and Animal Studies." *Hormones and Behavior* 64, no. 2 (2013): 399–410.

Klump, Kelly L., Jessica L. Suisman, Alexandra Burt, Matt McGue, and William G. Iacono. "Genetic and Environmental Influences on Disordered Eating: An Adoption Study." *Journal of Abnormal Psychology* 118 (November 2009): 797–805.

Lamoureux, Mary M. H., and Joan L. Bottorff. "'Becoming the Real Me': Recovering from Anorexia Nervosa." *Health Care for Women International* 26, no. 2 (2005): 170–88.

Lappé, Frances Moore. *Diet for a Small Planet.* New York: Ballantine, 1971.

Lawrence, Marilyn. *The Anorexic Mind.* London: Karnac, 2007.

———. "Body, Mother, Mind: Anorexia, Femininity and the Intrusive Object." *International Journal of Psychoanalysis* 83, no. 4 (2002): 837–50.

Levenkron, Steven. *The Best Little Girl in the World.* Chicago: Contemporary Books, 1978.

———. *Treating and Overcoming Anorexia Nervosa.* New York: Grand Central, 1988.

Levin, Eric. "Starved to a Tragic Death: A Sweet Surface Hid a Troubled Soul in the Late Karen Carpenter, a Victim of Anorexia Nervosa." *People,* February 21, 1983. http://www.people.com/people/archive/article/0,,20084327,00 .html.

Liu, Aimee. *Gaining: The Truth about Life after Eating Disorders.* New York: Grand Central, 2008.

Lock, James, ed. *The Oxford Handbook of Child and Adolescent Eating Disorders: Developmental Perspectives.* New York: Oxford University Press USA, 2012.

Long, Harland William. *Sane Sex Life, Sane Sex Living: Some Things That All Sane People Ought to Know about Sex Nature and Sex Functioning; Its Place in the Economy of Life, Its Proper Training and Righteous Exercise.* Boston: Badger, 1919.

McCarty, Jim. "Chillicothe's Slice of History: Sliced Bread Began Here in 1928." *Chillicothe Constitution Tribune,* September 2006. http://www.chillico thecity.org/bread/breadnews1.html.

Mclean, Sian A., Susan J. Paxton, and Eleanor H. Wertheim. "A Body Image and Disordered Eating Intervention for Women in Midlife: A Randomized Controlled Trial." *Journal of Psychological Science* 79, no. 6 (2011): 751–58.

Merino, Gustavo Gutierrez. *A Theology of Liberation.* 1971. Reprint, New York: Orbis, 1988.

Michigan State University. "Genetic Risk Factors for Eating Disorders Discovered." *ScienceDaily,* May 12, 2007. https://www.sciencedaily.com/relea ses/2007/05/070511150158.htm.

Minuchin, Salvador, Bernice L. Rosman, and Lester Baker. *Psychosomatic Families: Anorexia Nervosa in Context.* Cambridge: Harvard University Press, 1978.

National Eating Disorders Association. "Research on Males and Eating Disorders." https://www.nationaleatingdisorders.org/ research-males-and-eating-disorders.

Oates, Joyce Carol. "Adventures in Abandonment." Review of *Jean Stafford: A Biography,* by David Roberts. *New York Times,* August 28, 1988. http://www .nytimes.com/1988/08/28/books/adventures-in-abandonment.html.

Oberndorfer, Tyson A., K. W. Frank Guido, Alan N. Simmons, Angela Wagner, Andyale McCurdy, Julie L. Fudge, Tony T. Yang, Martin P. Paulus, and Walter H. Kaye. "Altered Insula Response to Sweet Taste Processing after Recovery from Anorexia and Bulimia Nervosa." *American Journal of Psychiatry* 170, no. 10 (2013): 1143–51.

Penn, Nathaniel. "The Growing Problem of Male Anorexia." *GQ,* September 13, 2012. http://www.gq.com/story/male-anorexia-gq-september-2012.

Petroff, Elizabeth Alvilda. *Medieval Women's Visionary Literature.* New York and Oxford: Oxford University Press, 1986.

Pike, Kathleen M., B. T. Walsh, K. Vitousek, G. T. Wilson, and J. Bauer. "Cognitive Behavior Therapy in the Posthospitalization Treatment of Anorexia Nervosa." *American Journal of Psychiatry* 160 (2003): 2046–49.

Raymond of Capua. *The Life of Catherine of Siena.* Completed in 1395. Wilmington, DE: Michal Glazier, 1980.

Reba-Harrelson, L., A. Von Holle, R. M. Hamer, R. Swann, M. L. Reyes, and Cynthia M. Bulik. "Patterns and Prevalence of Disordered Eating and Weight Control Behaviors in Women Ages 25–45." *Eating and Weight Disorders: Studies on Anorexia, Bulimia and Obesity* 14, no. 4 (December 2009): 190–98.

Rizzo, Mary. "Revolution in a Can: Food, Class, and Radicalism in the Minnesota Co-op Wars of the 1970s." In *Eating in Eden: Food and American Utopias,* ed. Etta M. Madden and Martha L. Finch, 220–38. Lincoln: University of Nebraska Press, 2006.

Rodin, Judith, Lisa Silberstein, and Ruth Striegel-Moore. "Women and Weight: A Normative Discontent." In *Nebraska Symposium on Motivation,* vol. 32, *Psychology and Gender,* ed. Theo B. Sonderegger, 267–307. Lincoln: University of Nebraska Press, 1984.

Rosen, Megan. "The Anorexic Brain: Neuroimaging Improves Understanding of Eating Disorder." *ScienceNews,* July 26, 2013. https://www.sciencenews.org/article/anorexic-brain.

Rosenfeld, Stacey M. *Does Every Woman Have an Eating Disorder? Challenging Our Nation's Fixation with Food and Weight.* Los Angeles: Siena Moon, 2014.

Roszak, Theodore. *The Making of a Counter Culture: Reflections on the Technocratic Society and Its Youthful Opposition.* New York: Doubleday, 1969.

Saukko, Paula. *The Anorexic Self: A Personal, Political Analysis of a Diagnostic Discourse.* Albany: State University Press of New York, 2008.

Schmidt, Randy L. *Little Girl Blue: The Life of Karen Carpenter.* Atlanta: A Cappella Books/Chicago Review Press, 2011.

"The Self-Starvers." *Time,* July 28, 1975, 30–31.

Strigo, Irina A., Scott C. Matthews, Alan N. Simmons, Tyson Oberndorfer, Megan Klabunde, Lindsay E. Reinhardt, and Walter H. Kaye. "Altered Insula Activation during Pain Anticipation in Individuals Recovered from Anorexia Nervosa: Evidence of Interoceptive Dysregulation." *International Journal of Eating Disorders* 46, no. 1 (2013): 22–33.

Tenneson, Joyce. *Wise Women: A Celebration of Their Insights, Courage, and Beauty.* New York: Bulfinch, 2002.

Tharp-Taylor, Shannah. "Anorexia in Blacks Gets New Scrutiny: Disorder May Not Be Rare as Thought." *Chicago Tribune,* August 25, 2003. http://articles.chicagotribune.com/2003-08-25/news/0308250246_1_anorexia-nervosa-disorders-african-american.

Thomas, Jennifer J., and Jenni Schaefer. *Almost Anorexic: Is My (or My Loved One's) Relationship with Food a Problem?* Center City, MN: Hazelden, 2013.

Vandereycken, Walter. "Dealing with Denial in Anorexia Nervosa." *Eating Disorders Review* 17, no. 6 (2006): 1.

Weil, Simone. *Waiting for God.* New York: Harper Perennial Modern Classics, 2009.

Weir, Kirsten. "New Insights on Eating Disorders." *Monitor on Psychology* (American Psychological Association), 47, no. 4 (2016): 36. http://www.apa.org/monitor/2016/04/eating-disorders.aspx.

Wolf, Naomi. *The Beauty Myth: How Images of Beauty Are Used against Women.* New York: Morrow, 1991.